First World War
and Army of Occupation
War Diary
France, Belgium and Germany

21 DIVISION
64 Infantry Brigade
King's Own (Yorkshire Light Infantry)
10th Battalion
11 January 1915 - 31 January 1918

WO95/2162/2

The Naval & Military Press Ltd
www.nmarchive.com
Published in association with The National Archives

Published by

The Naval & Military Press Ltd

Unit 10 Ridgewood Industrial Park,

Uckfield, East Sussex,

TN22 5QE England

Tel: +44 (0) 1825 749494

www.naval-military-press.com

www.nmarchive.com

This diary has been reprinted in facsimile from the original. Any imperfections are inevitably reproduced and the quality may fall short of modern type and cartographic standards.

© **Crown Copyright**
Images reproduced by permission of The National Archives, London, England, 2015.

Contents

Document type	Place/Title	Date From	Date To
Heading	WO95/2162-2		
Heading	10th Bn K.O.Y.L.I. Sep 1915-Jan 1918		
Heading	10th Battn. The King's Own Yorkshire Light Infantry. September (11.9.15 to 30.9.15) 1915		
War Diary	Witley Camp	11/09/1915	11/09/1915
War Diary	Southampton	11/09/1915	11/09/1915
War Diary	Havre	12/09/1915	13/09/1915
War Diary	Zutkerque	14/09/1915	20/09/1915
War Diary	Arques	21/09/1915	21/09/1915
War Diary	Fontes	22/09/1915	24/09/1915
War Diary	Four des Chaux	25/09/1915	25/09/1915
War Diary	Loos	26/09/1915	26/09/1915
War Diary	Philosophie	27/09/1915	28/09/1915
War Diary	Lignes Lez Aire	29/09/1915	30/09/1915
Heading	21st Division 10th K.O.Y.L.I. Vol 2 Oct 15		
War Diary	Lignes Lez Aire	01/10/1915	01/10/1915
War Diary	Boeseghem	02/10/1915	02/10/1915
War Diary	Rouge Croix	03/10/1915	10/10/1915
War Diary	Papot	11/10/1915	11/10/1915
War Diary	Ploegsteert	12/10/1915	12/10/1915
War Diary	Mud Lane Barricades	13/10/1915	15/10/1915
War Diary	Ploegsteert	16/10/1915	24/10/1915
War Diary	Bailleull	24/10/1915	24/10/1915
War Diary	Merris	25/10/1915	31/10/1915
Heading	21st Division 10th K.O.Y.L.I. Vol 3 Nov 15		
War Diary	Merris	01/11/1915	10/11/1915
War Diary	Bailleul	11/11/1915	12/11/1915
War Diary	Armentieres	13/11/1915	17/11/1915
War Diary	Houplines	18/11/1915	23/11/1915
War Diary	Le Tissage	24/11/1915	24/11/1915
War Diary	Tissage	25/11/1915	29/11/1915
War Diary	Trenches	30/11/1915	30/11/1915
Heading	21st Div 10th K.O.Y.L.I. Vol 4 December 1915		
War Diary	Trenches	01/12/1915	05/12/1915
War Diary	Armentieres	06/12/1915	11/12/1915
War Diary	Trenches	12/12/1915	18/12/1915
War Diary	Houplines	19/12/1915	26/12/1915
War Diary	Trenches	26/12/1915	29/12/1915
War Diary	Armentieres	30/12/1915	31/12/1915
Heading	10th K O Y L I 1916		
Heading	10th K.O.Y.L.I Vol 5		
War Diary	Armentieres	01/01/1916	04/01/1916
War Diary	Trenches	05/01/1916	10/01/1916
War Diary	Houplines	11/01/1915	16/01/1915
War Diary	Trenches	17/01/1916	23/01/1916
War Diary	Armentiers	23/01/1916	28/01/1916
War Diary	Houplines	29/01/1916	31/01/1916
War Diary	Trenches	01/02/1916	08/02/1916
War Diary	Houplines	09/02/1916	13/02/1916
War Diary	Armentieres	14/02/1916	19/02/1916

War Diary	Trench 67/71	20/02/1916	29/02/1916
Heading	10 K.O.Y.L.I. Vol I March 1916		
War Diary	Armentieres	01/03/1916	08/03/1916
War Diary	Trenches	09/03/1916	14/03/1916
War Diary	Armentieres	15/03/1916	18/03/1916
War Diary	Meteren	19/03/1916	29/03/1916
War Diary	La Neuville	30/03/1916	01/04/1916
War Diary	Buire	02/04/1916	04/04/1916
War Diary	Maulte	08/03/1916	14/03/1916
War Diary	La Neuville	15/03/1916	16/03/1916
War Diary	Ville	23/04/1916	02/05/1916
War Diary	Buire	12/05/1916	12/05/1916
War Diary	La Neuville	13/05/1916	24/05/1916
War Diary	Buire	24/05/1916	31/05/1916
War Diary	Meaulte	01/06/1916	04/06/1916
War Diary	Trenches	06/06/1916	13/06/1916
War Diary	Le Neuville	14/06/1916	18/06/1916
War Diary	Ribemont	19/06/1916	20/06/1916
War Diary	Buire	21/06/1916	30/06/1916
Heading	10th Battn. The King's Own (Yorkshire Light Infantry). July 1916		
War Diary	Trenches	01/07/1916	02/07/1916
War Diary	Dernacourt	03/07/1916	04/07/1916
War Diary	La Chaussee	04/07/1916	06/07/1916
War Diary	Mesge	07/07/1916	09/07/1916
War Diary	On Route To Ville	10/07/1916	10/07/1916
War Diary	Ville	11/07/1916	12/07/1916
War Diary	Trenches	13/07/1916	17/07/1916
War Diary	Meaulte	18/07/1916	19/07/1916
War Diary	On Route To Dreuil	20/07/1916	20/07/1916
War Diary	Dreuil	21/07/1916	22/07/1916
War Diary	On Route to Houvin	23/07/1916	23/07/1916
War Diary	Houvin	24/07/1916	28/07/1916
War Diary	Noyellette	29/07/1916	31/07/1916
Miscellaneous	Appendix I.		
Operation(al) Order(s)	Operation Order 6 By Lieut Colonel King Commanding 10th Bn. K.O.Y.L.I. Appendix.I.		
Heading	10th Battalion King's Own Yorkshire Light Infantry August 1916		
War Diary	Duisans	01/08/1916	04/08/1916
War Diary	Trenches	05/08/1916	10/08/1916
War Diary	Brigade Reserve	11/08/1916	15/08/1916
War Diary	Trenches	16/08/1916	22/08/1916
War Diary	Duisans	23/08/1916	28/08/1916
War Diary	Trenches	29/08/1916	31/08/1916
Heading	64th Brigades 21st Division 10th Battalion King's Own Yorkshire Light Infantry September 1916		
War Diary	Trenches	01/09/1916	04/09/1916
War Diary	Agnez-Les-Duisans	05/09/1916	05/09/1916
War Diary	Izel-Le-Hameau	06/09/1916	11/09/1916
War Diary	Houvin-Houvigneul	12/09/1916	12/09/1916
War Diary	Frevent	13/09/1916	13/09/1916
War Diary	Dernacourt	14/09/1916	15/09/1916
War Diary	Pomieres Redoubt	16/09/1916	16/09/1916
War Diary	Flers Trench	17/09/1916	17/09/1916
War Diary	Pomieres Redoubt	18/09/1916	18/09/1916

War Diary	Fricourt Camp	19/09/1916	21/09/1916
War Diary	Bernafay Wood	22/09/1916	22/09/1916
War Diary	Flers	23/09/1916	25/09/1916
War Diary	Goudecourt	26/09/1916	26/09/1916
War Diary	Bernafay Wood	27/09/1916	29/09/1916
War Diary	Ribemont	30/09/1916	30/09/1916
Miscellaneous	Major C.A. Milward, Indian Army. G.S.O.2. 20th (Light) Division.		
Heading	War Diary of 10th K.O.Y.L.I. for Month of October 16 Vol 14		
War Diary	Ribemont	01/10/1916	03/10/1916
War Diary	Bellancourt	04/10/1916	07/10/1916
War Diary	Allouagne	08/10/1916	10/10/1916
War Diary	Bethune	11/10/1916	11/10/1916
War Diary	Trenches (R Cambrian Sector)	14/10/1916	17/10/1916
War Diary	Support Trenches	18/10/1916	19/10/1916
War Diary	L Cambrian Sector	21/10/1916	21/10/1916
War Diary	Annequin	27/10/1916	31/10/1916
Heading	War Diary Of 10th Bn. K.O.Y.L.I. From 1st Nov to 30th Nov /16 Vol 15		
War Diary	Annequin	01/11/1916	01/11/1916
War Diary	Trenches	02/11/1916	06/11/1916
War Diary	Village Line	08/11/1916	09/11/1916
War Diary	Trenches	12/11/1916	12/11/1916
War Diary	Annequin	16/11/1916	17/11/1916
War Diary	Trenches	20/11/1916	20/11/1916
War Diary	Village Line	24/11/1916	29/11/1916
War Diary	La Bourse	30/11/1916	30/11/1916
Heading	10th Bn. K.O.Y.L.I. War Diary for December 1916 Vol 16		
War Diary	In Rest	01/12/1916	06/12/1916
War Diary	Bethune	07/12/1916	14/12/1916
War Diary	Trenches	15/12/1916	19/12/1916
War Diary	Reserve	22/12/1916	27/12/1916
War Diary	Fouquereuil	28/12/1916	28/12/1916
War Diary	Wormhoudt	29/01/1917	10/02/1917
War Diary	Esquelbecq	11/02/1917	11/02/1917
War Diary	Bethune	12/02/1917	12/02/1917
War Diary	Annequin	13/02/1917	13/02/1917
War Diary	Trenches	14/02/1917	19/02/1917
War Diary	Annequin	20/02/1917	23/02/1917
War Diary	Trenches	24/02/1917	06/03/1917
War Diary	Robecq	07/03/1917	09/03/1917
War Diary	Bourecq	10/03/1917	18/03/1917
War Diary	Ivergny	19/03/1917	23/03/1917
War Diary	Pommera	24/03/1917	28/03/1917
War Diary	Adinfer	29/03/1917	30/03/1917
War Diary	Boisleux au Mont	31/03/1917	31/03/1917
Heading	10th Battn K.O.Y.L.I. War Diary, April, 1917		
War Diary	Boisleux Au Mont	01/04/1917	11/04/1917
War Diary	Baing Becquerelle	11/04/1917	13/04/1917
War Diary	Ficheux	14/04/1917	19/04/1917
War Diary	Boisleux Au Mont	20/04/1917	25/04/1917
War Diary	Front Line	26/04/1917	30/04/1917
War Diary	In the Line	01/05/1917	26/05/1917
War Diary	Bellacourt	28/05/1917	31/05/1917

War Diary	Boyelles	01/06/1917	08/06/1917
War Diary	Front Line	09/06/1917	12/06/1917
War Diary	Boyelles	13/06/1917	20/06/1917
War Diary	Pommier	21/06/1917	29/06/1917
War Diary	Moyenneville	30/06/1917	30/06/1917
War Diary	Support Line Right Sector of Drive Front	01/07/1917	04/07/1917
War Diary	Front Line	04/07/1917	08/07/1917
War Diary	Moyenneville	04/07/1917	31/07/1917
War Diary	Support Line Right Sector	01/08/1917	06/08/1917
War Diary	Front Line Centre Sector	07/08/1917	16/08/1917
War Diary	Patricia Camp	17/08/1917	25/08/1917
War Diary	Boisleux Au Mont	26/08/1917	27/08/1917
War Diary	Berneville	28/08/1917	16/09/1917
War Diary	Hendeghem	17/09/1917	23/09/1917
War Diary	Thieushouk	24/09/1917	30/09/1917
War Diary	La Clytte	01/10/1917	01/10/1917
War Diary	Scottish Wood	02/10/1917	06/10/1917
War Diary	Zillebeke Railway Embarkment	07/10/1917	31/10/1917
Miscellaneous	10th (S) Bn. King's Own Yorkshire Light Infantry.		
Miscellaneous	10th (S) Bn. K.O. Yorkshire L.I.	11/10/1917	11/10/1917
War Diary	Brewery Camp	01/11/1917	01/11/1917
War Diary	Zillebeke	02/11/1917	09/11/1917
War Diary	Brewery Camp	10/11/1917	12/11/1917
War Diary	Ottawa Camp	13/11/1917	21/11/1917
War Diary	Ecoivres	22/11/1917	09/12/1917
War Diary	Longavesnes	10/12/1917	26/12/1917
War Diary	Heudecourt	27/12/1917	31/12/1917
War Diary	Saulcourt	31/12/1917	08/01/1918
War Diary	Epehy	09/01/1918	16/01/1918
War Diary	Saulcourt	17/01/1918	31/01/1918

washroom 2/2/62

21ST DIVISION
64TH INFY BDE

10TH BN K. O. Y. L. I.
SEP 1915 - JAN 1918

Disbanded

64th Inf.Bde.
21st Div.

Battn. disembarked
Havre from England
12.9.15.

WAR DIARY

10th BATTN. THE KING'S OWN YORKSHIRE LIGHT INFANTRY.

S E P T E M B E R

(11.9.15 to 30.9.15)

1 9 1 5

Jan '18

10th BATTALION K.O. YORKSHIRE L.I.
WAR DIARY.

DATE AND PLACE. SEPT. 1915		DETAIL.	REMARKS AND APPENDICES.
WITLEY CAMP	11 4.20AM	Entrained at MILFORD STA: Entrainment completed at 7.30 A.M. Arrived at SOUTHAMPTON:	Strength:- Officers 31 } 938. R&F 907
SOUTHAMPTON	11 10 P.M	Battalion completed disembarking at 10 A.M, and at 8.30 P.M. had all embarked in H.Q. Bn + transport under Lt.Col. A.W.C. Pollock in S/S "CALIFORNIA", remainder of Battalion under Maj. Ellis in S/S "EMPRESS QUEEN".	
HAVRE	12	Arrived at HAVRE 9.30 A.M. and completed disembarking at 12 noon. Marched to No 5 Rest Camp. Capt King, 2nd Lts 2 [?] Lee & Stoddart and 128	
HAVRE	12	men of "B" Company entrained at to Gare des Marchandises at 11 P.M. and left for AUDRINCQ.	
"	13	Remainder of Battalion entrained following day, arriving at AUDRINCQ at 10 A.M. and Marched into BULLS in village of ZUTKERQUE at 3 P.M.	
ZUTKERQUE	14	Route March 12 Miles	
"	15	Received orders to hand in at 3.15 P.M.x from Bn HQrs and were ready to move off at 6 P.M.	x Bomb-throwers + Bn S.O. also
"	16	Company training, S.A.A. Section and Snipers did front shooting	
"	17	Platoon French and Company training	x not accompanying Battalion

10th BATTALION K.O. YORKSHIRE L.I.
WAR DIARY.

DATE AND PLACE.			DETAIL.	REMARKS AND APPENDICES.
Sept. 16.15				
ZUTKERQUE:	17		Officers in charge proceeded into the trenches at 1am. Sept 17 1915 - In 24 hrs plan, returning to Billets at 1am. Sept. 17 1915	Onas. Atkinson. Capt. Dale Lieut. Sheffield. Lieut. Larkin 2nd Lieut. Burkett.
"	18	6.30 PM	Lt. Col. Pollock joined Quarters at NORDAUSQUE & proceeded to Front to inspect Trench Lines.	
"	19		Tactical Divisional Exercise near ZUTKERQUE. At 11 PM, Received orders to proceed to Ormr Smith (Division) Be ready to move out 5 PM. 20.9.15.	
"	20	5.15 PM	Marched out of ZUTKERQUE to ARQUES about 16 miles. Arrived 12 AM and went into close billets.	
ARQUES	21	7.30 PM	Marched out of ARQUES, arriving at FONTES at 1 AM. Twelve miles. Went into close Billets	
FONTES	22	7.30 PM	Marched out of FONTES, arriving at AMES at 9.30 PM. And went into Billets.	
"	23		Rest Day. Returned all Blankets to Rail-Head for delivery to ORDNANCE BASE	7 Men in Hospital to date. Weather v. fine since arrival in FRANCE.
"	24		The two Argentine mules both have twin of mules on 20.9.15 journey the Batt., during the night	

10th BATTALION K.O. YORKSHIRE L.I.
WAR DIARY.

DATE AND PLACE.		DETAIL.	REMARKS AND APPENDICES.
FOUR du CHAUX. Sept. 25	1 AM	Bivouacked in fields with remainder of Brigade until 12 noon when the Bde. moved off to trenches in front of Loos. The Bn. arrived just before daybreak and occupied a line of old (?) German trenches about 3/4 mile N.W. of Loos, with the 9 KOYLI on LEFT and D.L.I. Bn. Cty in on left front. TRENCHES were under shell fire all day and at 1PM, other attacks having failed, the 10 Bn were ordered themselves to move out bottom of Valley facing German Redoubt and to take up a position there in readiness to support the 9' Bn KOYLI who were assembling the Redoubt. Constant movement and at 4pm P.M. Bn returned under heavy shell fire to a line of old German trenches a mile in rear of the original line taken up the night before.	Capt. A.M. Stahl and Lieut. S/M & Capt. Goth performed acts of bravery and @ 26. The former [unclear] is already reported has ? of the latter were to him ? 700 [unclear] nominated S.A.A. ammunition into our trench under heavy shell fire with the exception of five men whose names are given below :- A/Serjt. WHITE. A.O.D. Driver THOMPSON 10Bde. TAYLOR B) Ammo. STEAD) drivers
LOOS. 26			
PHILOSOPHIE 27	@5 1AM the Batln. were relieved by units of GUARDS DIV and marched back in scattered detachments to bivouac at PHILOSOPHIE three miles behind the firing line. Capt Stahl was wounded by Shell fire about 2.30PM on 12th Sept 26 whilst scout Offr. rallying his Battn. after trenches [unclear] back to top of ridge. Capt. I.A. Don. Lieut. Stanfield, Lieuts. Stoddard were also wounded in Graces during the day and ? [men], 87 [?] were sent to hospital on 27 also suffered from severe bruising. Early in morning of 28/9/15 27. Cpl. AWA POLLOCK had the	
28			

10th BATTALION K.O. YORKSHIRE L.I.
WAR DIARY.

DATE AND PLACE.	DETAIL.	REMARKS AND APPENDICES.
Sept 28th	Eleven Whippet Tanks passing thro' the Street of Noeux Pernes. At 10 pm in pouring rain the Bn moved up from PHILOSOPHIE and entrained at NOEUX LES MINES	
LIGNES LEZ AIRE 29th	at 3 am detrained at BURBETTE and marched into LIGNES LES AIRES and billets arriving there at 11.30 am	48/ 48/
30th	Rest day. Spent in changing equipment of Lewis gun men into Waterproof suits in case Crait Gas	48/ 48/

64/21st Division

121/7430

10th K.O.Y.L.I.
vol 2

Oct 15

Apparently in fighting at Loos
Thurs 70 Wednes day very
little about it except that
he returned
24/10/16

10th BATTALION K.O. YORKSHIRE L.I.
WAR DIARY.

DATE AND PLACE.	DETAIL.	REMARKS AND APPENDICES.
LIGNES LES AIRE 1916	Marched from LIGNES LES AIRE at 9.30 am and arrived at BOESEGHEM at 1pm. We went into billets in the night and left again at 9 am on 2nd. Having NE transpt. HAZEBROUCK arriving at ROUGE CROIX at 2 P.M. Weather fine. Billetting area very extended and great difficulty was experienced in getting the whole Bn. under cover.	
BOESEGHEM 2nd		
ROUGE CROIX	Sunday. Church Parade 9.30 am. and in the afternoon in showery afternoon.	

10th BATTALION K.O. YORKSHIRE L.I.
WAR DIARY.

DATE AND PLACE.	DATE Dec 1915	DETAIL.	REMARKS AND APPENDICES.
ROUGE CROIX	4	Parades under Company C/O. Inspection by O/C. of Arms equipment and rifles.	Nil.
"	5	Battn. Arms marched in Morning. Cleaned equipment afternoon.	Nil.
"	6	Company Parades and Jnst-Mobilisation. Later this am. one ten minute all Companies and Sport nearly to move off. Lieut A.V. SCUDAMORE accidentally shot himself with revolver in leg and went to Hospital. 2/Lt. F.H. LEE went to hospital with Influenza.	Remained.
"	7	Battn: Inspected by Brig-General Walker and Sir Herbert Plumer. Satisfactory. Draft of nr hundred and forty men including two Sergeants arrived in 6 from 11th Battn. Very good lot of men.	Nil. Fine.
"	8	Marched to BAILLEUL and went into Billets.	Nil.
"	9	Marched out of BAILLEUL at 2.30 P.M. to PAPOT. Relieved one Platoon of each Coy into trenches occupied by 8 (B.) R.W.R. Regt.	Nil.
"	10	Four Platoons were relieved and 2 of his-in-line sent up in their place. C/o. and Adjutant spent all day looking over trenches. Decided they were good & each day but required a good deal of work on them.	Enemy very quiet and but for a few Shrapnel Shells little fire from their lines. Our Guns were firing active all day.

10th BATTALION K.O. YORKSHIRE L.I. WAR DIARY.

DATE AND PLACE.		DETAIL.	REMARKS AND APPENDICES.
PAPOT.	11	Shelling off continuing. C/O and Adjutant in trenches during the morning. Three German aeroplanes overhead the whole morning, heavily fired upon by our guns with no result.	Nil.
PLOEGSTEERT MUD LANE BARRICADES.	12	All platoons back from trenches in camp.	Nil.
	13	Received orders to take over trenches in PLOEGSTEERT WOOD from 8' K.O. LANCASTERS. Relief to commence at 9 P.M. The night was very black and after rain the ground very slippery. 2 bat Platoon got in well and every wire very good, took a stream of trolls began to cover our H.qrs suddenly arrived at Parapet of our fire trench and having crossed this dropped down his Relief was complete at 11.25 A.M in thick damp mist. Day passed quietly, our guns occasionally shelling Enemy dropped a few shrapnel shells near BARRICADES doing no afternoon without damage.	
	14	Enemy artillery active at times; two Shrapnel dropped in rear of A Coy support trench, killed one man and wounded two others.	Nil.
	15	6.P.M. Enemy rifle grenade landed in Bay 38 Trench 12S. took off head of Pt. J.W. LUCKMAN who was in M.S. Emplacement with LEWIS GUN. Cpl D.H. WINGHAM had a narrow escape.	Nil.

10th BATTALION K.O. YORKSHIRE L.I.
WAR DIARY.

DATE AND PLACE.		DETAIL.	REMARKS AND APPENDICES.
PLOEGSTEERT	Oct		
	16	Quiet night. Desultory Rifle fire only. Enemy kept sending up flares and were evidently nervous. Believe a himnet is being brought towards our trenches opposite junction of 125/124. Patrols of our own went out reported that enemy were extremely diligging underground about 150 yards from our own trench. We have commenced occupying here the last three nights kept been very foggy and dark. The men are settling down to the work well.	Various working parties out all day repairing parapets & returning width of trenches. Wire parties going out at night out Patrols. Sup. THAM F. wounded in D. Coy. S.2. at 5 p.m. in leg.
	17	Quiet day, no men wounded in trench.	HQ
	18	Enemy quiet until evening. At 4.P.M. commenced shelling PLOEG STEERT WOOD and the STRAND. WIT BANES. Month, at times our guns replied and about 6.30 P.M. firing died down to nil.	HQ
	19	Relieved by 15 R.L.I. and Battalion marched back to PIOGGRIEFS liso Remainder of Bath. Giving huts Bde. Reserve. Reliefs were carried out without mishap.	HQ
	20	Two hundred men on fatigue work Working Parties, improving and repairing Communication Trenches.	HQ
	21	Three companies proceeded to LE BIZET to Bathe.	HQ
	22		HQ
	23	Working Parties out under R.E.	HQ

… 10th BATTALION K.O. YORKSHIRE L.I.

WAR DIARY.

DATE AND PLACE. October 15		DETAIL.	REMARKS AND APPENDICES.
PLOEGSTEERT	24	Relieved by 3rd Worcester Regt. up from LA HOOGE and battalion marched into BAILLEUL having spent nine days actually in front line trenches and nine days in Battn: in Reserve.	H.Q.
BAILLEUL	25	Marched into BAILLEUL at 3 P.M. and went into Billets for night.	H.Q.
MERRIS	25	Marched into MERRIS 12 noon, heavy rain & went into billets in farm houses.	H.Q.
	26	Rest march and cleaning up.	H.Q.
	27	Attachment of Subalterns and two Officers proceeded to BAILLEUL from 9th Reserve Battalion of the Bde. to be seen by H.M.	H.Q.
	28	Rest march and Company Drill	H.Q.
	29	Opened Rifle Range 100 yds. Two targets	H.Q.
	30	Rest Marching and Shooting.	Major Ellis Guest Hospital H.Q.
	31	Church Parade.	H.Q.

H.E. Hirosy
Major.

10th K.O.Y.L.I.
Vol: 3

74/24

L.A. 8.M.
5 sheets

21st Division

Nov. 15

10th BATTALION K.O. YORKSHIRE L.I.
WAR DIARY.

DATE AND PLACE		DETAIL.	REMARKS AND APPENDICES.
MERRIS	Nov. 1915 1st	Rain. Work continued of improving billets.	Bn. H.q. T.2 b.47 MAP. 36A 1/40000
"	2		Maj. Ellis returned from Hospital.
"	3	✗ Major W.B. STEWART arrived and took over command of Bn.	(LOTHIAN & BORDER HORSE) ^ 25° DIV:
"	4	Ordinary training. Work carried out, including	
"	5	trenching and Musketry work. Smokehelmets used for	WD
"	6	first time, after adjustment. Bn. fair shooting down 1 to 900. At full	WD
"	7	General Inspection command. T. Corps Inspected Battn.	WD
"	8	11 A.M. Parade numbers two officers and 950 other Ranks.	WD
"	9	During last few days equipment & supplies of all kinds have been arriving, and Battalion is now much better in respect for kits.	WD
BAILLEUL	10	Moved in BAILLEUL to billets. 11.45 AM.	WD
"	11	Short Route March	WD
"	12	Marched out for ARMENTIERES at 2.45 pm. Cold and Rain. Corps. at 1/2 mile intervals, precaution against shell fire, moved into Billets at ARMENTIERES at 6pm. About 9.45 P.M. part of these Billettings were shelled rather heavily. two shells dropped at D.Coys Billet, one man being very slightly wounded. A Battn. of N.F. close by lost six men killed.	WD
ARMENTIERES	13	400 Men in S. & SS. Trenches cleaning and repairing.	WD

10th BATTALION K.O. YORKSHIRE L.I.
WAR DIARY.

DATE AND PLACE.		DETAIL.	REMARKS AND APPENDICES.
ARMENTIERES	14	400 Opm at work repairing trench line. At times under shell fire. Two men slightly hit. Trenches in many places fallen in. And a great deal of work to be done. C/O, Adjutant and S.O. came round having shell fire near HOUPLINES DISTILLERY and had to go to ground for 1/2 hr.	
"	15	} Work carried on repairing trenches in S.S. line and subsidiary line	WW
"	16		WW
"	17		
HOUPLINES	18	Bath. took over the Trenches occupied by 15 D.L.I. first Coy. marched from HOUPLINES STA. at 5.30 a.m. Relief completed with exception of M.Gun Section at 9 a.m.	
	19	2/Lt. ATHOL JAMES ALLEN BYERLEY reported at 9.20 a.m.. Trenches very wet especially 89 and 85. Men working continually repairing Parapets. Dug outs and Communication Trenches.	WW Killed 1. Wounded 2 [1a] WW
	20	Weather gradually drying up and have just gotten the men more partially covered with cloaks and leather waistcoats. Very little shelling.	WW Wd 1. — 1 — 2 (1a) WW 1. — 1 — 3 WW
	22		
	23	Quiet day	
LETISSAGE.	24	Relieved by 15 D.L.I. Completed 8.30 a.m. Static 6.20 a.m. WW.	

10th BATTALION K.O. YORKSHIRE L.I. WAR DIARY.

DATE AND PLACE.		DETAIL.	REMARKS AND APPENDICES.
TISSAGE. Nov 1915	25	Large working parties out in trench line. Two lectures to officers	
	26	Work parties out as usual, shelled TISSAGE about 3.30 pm. 2 lectures to officers. Enemy shells thrown up by M.G. Anti-Aircraft guns.	
	27	Work parties. Lectures to officers. Lectures to officers	
	28	"	
	29	"	
TRENCHES	30	Took over front line trenches from 15 G.L. Antwerp ARMENTIERES branch shelled during night 29/30. Huns appear to have brought up some heavy guns to LILLE.	

(Signatures)

10 K.O.Y.L.I.

16th K.O.Y.L.I.
Vol: 4
December 1915

121/7931

R.S. A.M.
5 sheets

21/5/16

10th BATTALION K.O. YORKSHIRE L.I.
WAR DIARY.

DATE AND PLACE. Dec: 1915	DETAIL.	REMARKS AND APPENDICES.
TRENCHES. 1/3	Rain. Trenches feeling in and very wet, men all wonderfully cheerful. Dec. 2. Major AKROYD went to Hospital, Capt. Smith took over command of A. Coy.	Maj. AKROYD.
4	Enemy's Artillery somewhat active. Houghans very heavily shelled. Trenches very bad, men losing their gum and boots in the mud.	
5		
6	Relieved by 15' S.L.I. Relief started at 6.30 a.m. and were not completed until 12 pm, only two avenues available and men above their ankles in mud and water.	
ARMENTIERES 7/9	Two badly chilled on the 9" from 1.30 pm mud 3 pm. All men sent to cellars. One man slightly wounded.	
10	Baths inspected in billets by G.O.C. 21st DIV. Gen. JACOB and	
11	Working parties to front line trenches	
12	Started taking over trenches from 15' S.L.I. at 2.30 am (true hour Company left- HOOPLINES sta.), owing	
TRENCHES 13/14	to floods. Relief of 88, 89 and 85 went up by train no casualties. Enemy very quiet. Much description of Mr Guinness Thos. New very active, watching for M. in parapets was	

10th BATTALION K.O. YORKSHIRE L.I.
WAR DIARY.

DATE AND PLACE. DEC. 1915	DETAIL.	REMARKS AND APPENDICES.
TRENCHES 15	Nothing particular knocked down during.	
16	Heavy bombardment of Enemy's line S.W. of ARMENTIERES. Bombardment continued at 3.15 am. 8 Somersets relieved Enemy's line with one Company. Returned with few prisoners, one machine gun + two comrades. 13 CHESHIRE'S on our Left and 1st E.YORKS on our Right.	
17	Quiet day	
18	Relieved by 15th D.L.I. at daybreak. Battalion went into Support at HOUPLINES	
HOUPLINES 19	Gas attack by Huns on Front N.W. of YPRES at 5.45 am. At 6.30 Received warning Enemy blew up mine South of our in front of 65 Bde Trenches, little damage done. Very heavy bombardment heard in YPRES direction all through night.	
20	19/20. British claim that there attack Dec. 24 received. Work parties as usual.	
21/23	Relieved 15th D.L.I. in Trenches. No mine for three days.	
24	Xmas passed off very Quietly. No overtures of Friendships made by Turner or Foe. A	
25	good deal of night firing.	
26	Our troops very active all day. No reply from Turner. Evening raining	

15

10th BATTALION K.O. YORKSHIRE L.I.
WAR DIARY.

DATE AND PLACE.		DETAIL.	REMARKS AND APPENDICES.
Armentières Dec 1915	26	Coloured lights continuously. Wind due West, very quiet.	WWI
	27	Very quiet	WWI
	28	Battn. H.Qrs CAMBRIDGE HOUSE heavily shelled from LILLE direction from 10 am to 11 am. House very heavily damaged but cellars held up 5.9 Howitzer used and shrapnel. No casualties in the Battn. At 6.15 p.m. Aw Blm up mine in German parapet opposite sand 88, leaving unexploded with heavy rifle fire for a few minutes.	WWI
	29	Subdued by 15 S.A.A. Bands 66 and 87 heavily bombarded with 2 inch Trench Mortars and fire from direction of LILLE bearing 170°. Germans suffered considerable casualties.	WWI
Armentières	30	Work parties to the trenches as usual.	WWI
	31	2nd Lieut F. Weir reported for duty from ENGLAND 10.30 pm.	

W Bingham Lieut Col
Commanding
10th K.O.Y.L.I.

May Milward

10 KOYLI

1916

NOT FOR
VISITORS

10th K.O.Y.L.I.
Vol: 5

J.a 5.M.
     8 sheets

2/9

10th BATTALION K.O. YORKSHIRE L.I.
WAR DIARY.

DATE AND PLACE.		DETAIL.	REMARKS AND APPENDICES.
ARMENTIERES January 1916	1	Work Parties, Eng. on Duty, repair loading and trench fighting.	(WW)
	2	"	WW
	3	Baths and rest day	WW
	4	Work parties as usual	WW
	5	Relief completed by 9.30 am. Quiet	WW
TRENCHES	6	CAMBRIDGE HOUSE heavily shelled from 1700. No casualties during yesterdays shelling although the Huns put 100 6" and 8" shells HE 2/Lt. AMIEN & 2/Lt A.C. COCKCROFT joined into the house	WW, WW, WW
	7	Quiet day. Line. Wind N.W.	WW
	8	Quiet day. Sent JASKIE to evacuated trench any more	WW
	9	Ellis became the Bath, preceeding trench.	WW
	10	Quiet day in trenches.	WW
HOUPLINES	11	Relieved by 15 DLI. Heavy bombardment of enemys trenches from 11-2pm. HOUPLINES very heavily shelled by enemy. Church and Ruin	WW
	11	Bge of LYS at C.21.d.4.4. Church on fire: Quiet day. 62" Bty in us fight brought off a human demonstration in the August from 11/12. Our German prisoners were taken and about 200 WW	WW
	12		

10th BATTALION K.O. YORKSHIRE L.I.
WAR DIARY.

DATE AND PLACE.		DETAIL.	REMARKS AND APPENDICES.
	Aug 1916		
HOUPLINES	12	Enemy reported hostile. Retaliation in part of enemy very slight. Operation commenced at 11.15 pm and party were back in our line at 11.40 pm. Our party suffered some casualties. Carried work parties.	NIL
	13	"	"
	14	"	"
	15	"	"
	16	"	"
TRENCHES	17	Relieved 1/5 D.L.I., relief complete by 6.30 am.	NIL
	18	Quiet day.	"
	19	Trenches greatly improved: 2/5 Div. on our left attacked LE TOUQUET Salient under cover of a smoke cloud. Our Artillery bombarded the Salient trenches all day, and attack was launched at 4.45 pm. Enemy fairly quiet: fifty men in raid at ARMENTIERES preparing for raid in German our Trenches.	NIL
ARMENTIERES	20/22:		
	23	Relieved by 1/5 D.L.I. in 23rd inst., rest of epidemic was quieter.	NIL

10th BATTALION K.O. YORKSHIRE L.I.
WAR DIARY.

DATE AND PLACE.		DETAIL.	REMARKS AND APPENDICES.
ARMENTIERES	24	Work parties as usual.	W.W.
	25	At 9.55 pm. 4 officers and 53 R.& F. entered the German trenches at C.17. c.7.8, point of the penta crossed one German Sand without being observed and found the German front line un-occupied. Both extremities of the enemy's trench were blocked up and no progress could be made. At 10.11 pm. the whole party were clear of the German Parapet and were looking after in a deep ditch. Our army between the lines. Few shots stayed until the enemy shell fire in our front line and support trenches had abated. The whole party were back in our trenches by 11 pm. Casualties: 2/Lt Cockcroft. Wounded accidentally in the right arm. The Div. Artillery cut the enemy wire this day, previous to the raid very successfully. They also	

10th BATTALION K.O. YORKSHIRE L.I.
WAR DIARY.

DATE AND PLACE.	DETAIL.	REMARKS AND APPENDICES.
26.	established a curtain of fire, which effectually prevented any interference on the part of the enemy's infantry. Artillery Curtain of fire came into operation on the Moment the Raiding Party entered the Trenches and was continued until 10.20 p.m: (1) Enemy's Artillery did not open until ten pm and then their fire fell heavily on our front line Trenches and support lines, 7.7cm chiefly and about fifteen rounds H.E. dropped from a heavy gun (8") in direction of LOMME. (2) Casualties were inflicted on the 15 S.L.I. who were holding the Trenches at the time. (3) The Very Cordial assistance given by the 15 S.L.I. were very noticeable and notwithstanding the very heavy Artillery retaliation, they sent up regular bursts of rapid fire in spite of great difficulties, and gave all assistance in their power both before, during and after the raid. (WWW)	Officers. Capt. H.K. KING Lieut. A.I. HARISON 2 Lieut. H. BURKETT " A.C. COCKCROFT.

10th BATTALION K.O. YORKSHIRE L.I.
WAR DIARY.

DATE AND PLACE.		DETAIL.	REMARKS AND APPENDICES.
Armentieres	26	Work parties in day. Battalion dinner in evening at No 35 Rue Nationale. The first social meeting we have had since we left England. The CO proposed "A long life & a peaceful one" for the Staves. Ashley mannum.	
"	27 & 28	1 NCO and 19 men DRAFT from HULL (per) Work parties as usual. The Adjutant left for 10 days trousering on leave.	MM Draft 20 MM MM
Houplines	29	Owing to extensive damage done by hostile artillery to communication trenches, the relief was denied out this morning under cover of dark. it was completed at 16.0 am. Enemy artillery has been hardly active in the last three or three days and some flats of our trenches (especially B1) are literally unrecognisable. The enemy have been sending over a good deal of heavy shell today but little damage done.	MM.

10th BATTALION K.O. YORKSHIRE L.I.
WAR DIARY.

DATE AND PLACE.		DETAIL.	REMARKS AND APPENDICES.
Houplines	Jan. 30	Heavy mist. Front quiet all day. Wind in the East.	WW.
"	31.	The G.O.C. 21st Div visited the front line today. Enemy very quiet.	W Forster Newport 2/Col Capt. 10th KOYLI

10th BATTALION K.O. YORKSHIRE L.I.
WAR DIARY.

DATE AND PLACE 1916		DETAIL.	REMARKS AND APPENDICES.
TRENCHES Feby	1/7	After Hostile artillery activity of the previous few days, things have quietened down considerably. In the night of the 6/7, the flame thrower in one of our galleries in front of trench 88, about 20 yds from German lines was exploded accidentally. Quiet day.	Draft of 7 N.C.O.s and 6 Pts from ETAPLES.
	8	Relieved by 9 K.O.Y.L.I. The Battn. going into Bde. Reserve on HOUPLINES.	
HOUPLINES.	9	Work Parties as usual.	
	10		2/Lt. L.E.J. MAUDE joined
	11		
	12		Captain J. SHEFFIELD rejoined
	13	HOUPLINES RIVER BRIDGE area surrounding heavily shelled by S"H.E. from 9.30am from direction of LORGIES, about half of fire shell being two minutes.	Lieut J. SHEFFIELD surrendered
ARMENTIERES	14	Battn. were relieved by 2 Bn. MIDDX. Regt. at 10pm	
	15	Work Parties as usual.	
	16	C/O. Adjutant and Coy O/C went over trenches 67/70 & in trenches MUSHROOM preliminary reconnaissance in	
	17	Fine day.	
	18	Work Parties as usual.	
	19	Battn. relieved 13 N.F. in Trenches 66/71, MUSHROOM	

10th BATTALION K.O. YORKSHIRE L.I.
WAR DIARY.

DATE AND PLACE.		DETAIL.	REMARKS AND APPENDICES.
TRENCH 67/71	20	3 MILES South East of ARMENTIERES. Enemy very quiet.	
	21/22	Enemys Machine guns active nightly, otherwise attitude quiet. Wind unvarying E.N.E. Capt BETHELL killed in morning of 21/22 in night communication trench to MUSHROOM, whilst attending his men. A fine example in the highest sense of communication trench.	Capt. BETHELL killed
	23	At 5.30am the Huns opened a heavy trench-mortar & rifle grenade fire on SPAIN AVENUE and subsequent fire on suspected for 15 minute point. Very heavy shells being thrown in.	
	24	11pm 65 "Bde attempted a Minor Operation against BLACK REDOUBT. A party of 30 got into the German wire but were driven back by grenades.	
	25	Relieved at 9pm by 1st E. YORKS, Batt'n then took over Subsidiary line from LILLE Road.	2/Lt WILCHER ground
	26	Town of BUTERNE.	
	27	Quiet day. Work parties as ordered.	
	28		

10th BATTALION K.O. YORKSHIRE L.I.
WAR DIARY.

DATE AND PLACE.	DETAIL.	REMARKS AND APPENDICES.
1915 July 20	Arrived into billets at ARMENTIERES as 10 p.m. 28 Rue Faid Herbe. Relieved in subsection held by 1st S.L.I.	W Burton Leonard Lt Col Cmg 10=KOYLI

21
10 KOYLI
WMZ
March 1916

J.M.
4 sheets

10/KOYLI

10th BATTALION K.O. YORKSHIRE L.I.
WAR DIARY.

March 1916

DATE AND PLACE.		DETAIL.	REMARKS AND APPENDICES.
ARMENTIERES	1	Work parties as usual	Officers sig[nal]ling soft.
	2	Moved to Billets in Rue SADI CARNOT.	soft.
	3	Decided to commence training extra Lewis Gunners and Grenadiers. Seems as tho' we cannot be in when our Batt. comes out to rest for nine days	soft.
	4	Officer that C in C has cancelled ordinary leave 2/Lt. Kennedy from heavily shelled between 2/LT. A.L. KENNEDY.	
	5	11.30 5 pm Shells mostly falling around Div. HQrs	soft.
	6	Quiet day	soft.
	7	Work parties as usual. Training "Number 89"	soft.
	8	M.G. Brigade Williams 1st in the Rest.	soft.
9/11		A very Quiet six days indeed. Enemy's fire in all three very light. Our Bde M.G. Coy Regimental for the first time during in - struck here or brings back the rifles. 6 Lt of Sussex took over post in by the Batim. was brought up fund and GOODWOOD	soft.
		Reconnoissance H.Q. Batim. HQrs	
ARMENTIERES	15		soft.

10th BATTALION K.O. YORKSHIRE L.I.
WAR DIARY.

DATE AND PLACE.		DETAIL.	REMARKS AND APPENDICES.
ARMENTIERES	18	Proceeded out to LA CRUCHE en route to NIEW. FRANCE.	J.S. Martyn
METEREN	19	Remained March and arrived at METEREN 10.15am. Billets. Sons huts and Billets.	J.S. Martyn
	20	Rest and recuperation in training. Parade work. Troops own church & short Route Marches. Lt Col Setherwood to hospital.	J.S. Martyn
	21		J.S. Martyn
	22/26	Company Drill, Route Marching etc. One Coy per day on Grenadier Work. Sir D. HAIG passed through DIV. AREA on 25. Weather v. Cold. Rain & snow.	J.S. Martyn
	27/29	Batt. Marched past Gen. PLUMER G.O.C. 2 ARMY, on OUTERSTEENE - BAILLEUL Rd. O.O. accordance to Moving South on 31.	Capt Molson. A.P. Lt Dugmore A.R. 2Lt Asher. K. 2Lt Beatson. M.R. From 11th Batt. 28/3/16 J.S. Martyn
LA NEUVILLE.	30/31	O.O. 35 Received from Bde that Div. would form XIII Corps. Battn. entrained at Tom at GODEWAERSVELDE and arrived at LONGUEAU at 6pm and Marched Immediately via CORBIE to LA NEUVILLE on Left bank of R. SOMME. a distance of 10 miles from AMIENS. Entrained 29 officers 821 other Ranks.	J.S. Martyn

J.S. Martyn

10th BATTALION K.O. YORKSHIRE L.I.
WAR DIARY.

DATE AND PLACE.		DETAIL.	REMARKS AND APPENDICES.
AMIENS.	1916 April		
LA NEUVILLE	1	Battn. moved to BUIRE-sur-l'ANCRE marched at 8 a.m. and arrived in billets at 12 noon.	
BUIRE.	2/4	Two men each day working on Railway at DERNANCOURT. Remainder Grenades work and drill	
MAULTÉ	8	Marched into MAULTÉ on morning of the 8. Battn. took over QUEEN'S REDOUBT, BONTÉ REDOUBT and the village of BERCORDEL BECOURT. Situated in rear of Front line W. of TRICOURT.	
	11	From 7pm – 8pm the Germans heavily bombarded the 8 Div. front on our left occupied by R.I.R. and R.B. Germans also reported to have broken into LA NEUVILLE on its East.	
LA NEUVILLE	12/14		
	15		
	16	All Grenadier Bombers on different trenches on English ground N. of PONT NOYELLES Rd.	
VILLE	23	Marched from LA NEUVILLE at 6am. Arrived VILLE 13 noon. From 16/23 so many men on parade were severed in attack on trenches.	

26

10th BATTALION K.O. YORKSHIRE L.I.
WAR DIARY.

APRIL

DATE AND PLACE.	DETAIL.	REMARKS AND APPENDICES.
VILLE	24/30. Baths & work, large parties on work parties day and night men	Villa Jqw

A.J.Ferry Lt.Col.
Comdg. 10 Bn. K.O.Y.L.I.
BEF. FRANCE

10th BATTALION K.O. YORKSHIRE L.I.
WAR DIARY.

January 1916

DATE AND PLACE.	DETAIL.	REMARKS AND APPENDICES.
VILLE 1		sgd.
2	Took over left half of front line of Division from PURFLEET – BECOURT WOOD. This morn the front line the Battn. had done a 10 days tour in the front line. The enemy's activity chiefly consisted of shell fire, trench mortars and a plentiful distribution of 1913 pattern Rifle grenades. On the night of 2nd 3. our Sappers blew up three mines in front of the "JAMBOUR" and our Battalion put up a 5 minutes barrage. Enemy retaliation was slight. Again on the night of 3rd 4 (Army Hqrs 34 Div.) about a working party on our left was enfiladed and bombarded its counter trenches for 30 minutes from 1.59 A.M – 2.20 P.M. Enemy retaliation with shell fire and on our front line and communication trenches suffered somewhat severely. Relieved by 8 Som. L.I. at 5 p.m. 12 mrs and marched to Billets in BUIRE	Casualties for ten days:— Killed O.R. 2 sgd. Wounded " 10 sgd.
BUIRE 12		
LANEVILLE 13	Marched to LANEVILLE and arrived in Billets at noon	sgd. sgd. sgd. 9.11. 3 sheets

10th BATTALION K.O. YORKSHIRE L.I. (21)
WAR DIARY.

Vol 9

DATE AND PLACE.		DETAIL.	REMARKS AND APPENDICES.
May			
La NEUVILLE	14/16	Practice work in trenches; Assault etc.	sgd
	17	Brigade less 1 E.YORKS practiced the Assault: Start line 9' & 10' KOYLI. 15 DLI in Support. Work good.	sgd
	18/19	Battn. paraded at 4.15 AM, 1 Route March, transferred out at 4.30 AM, via DOURS, FOUILLY – CORBIE. Lt. DUSMORE took on 16 Battn: Scouts and commenced a special training course with them.	sgd
	20/21	Battn. carried on Assault for the differential training from now on. 9.15 pm K.O.Y.L.I. Reveille 6 DAOURS Band went. Tower Warned from 7 to 7.15 sub AK 211 from left to 6 bogging lorries left at small Stream to KOYLI last by the night ? line. Glo. Vert 5 Parkway pd Ringo received in further trenches.	sgd
	22 23	0.6.44 Returns. Battn. moved into Div. Reserve Quarters from LA NEUVILLE on 6.30 AM 23 with	sgd sgd
	24	B Coy proceed to intermediate line furnishing garrisons on strong points and Automatic Redan. On the 22" 85 N.C.O.'s & but man of D	sgd

10th BATTALION K.O. YORKSHIRE L.I.
WAR DIARY.

DATE AND PLACE.		DETAIL.	REMARKS AND APPENDICES.
June 1916			
BURÉ	24	D Coy. proceeded to RIBEMONT on attached duty for working parties at MERICOURT &c. The Battalion less B and D Coy furnishing work parties day and night in and E1 MEAULTE. Draft of sixty three O.R. arrived from 3rd E. Battn.	sgd sgd DRAFT.
		POPERINGHE:	
	29/30/31	Work parties in several fronts and dans	Capt. A.L. KENNEDY, left to join GHQ. Intelly. Staff : sgd
July		In attacks P.S. B Coy furnished kits and men to Battalions 15, 16, 17, 18, 19 and 20. Relieved 2nd Lieut's in positions of H Middx. Regt. in front at 1. am	2/Lt SCUDAMORE reported for duties 30/5/16.

signatures

10th BATTALION K.O. YORKSHIRE L.I.
WAR DIARY.

June 1916

DATE AND PLACE.	DETAIL.	REMARKS AND APPENDICES.
MEAULTE 1	Marched into MEAULTE to form Bde Reserve. Front line 9 KOYLI, 1 E Yorks, 13 DLI, BERCORDEL and the Redoubts. 34 Div was in left sector. Enemy's artillery somewhat more active than usual intermittent shelling in and around town all day.	French Gazette. Military Medal. 21564 Pte CLARK. J.S. 20112 " ELLIS. E.
2		Casualties Killed Wounded
3		
3	Relieved 3/4 [?] Own. G. and gave for... UKE to division of LA BOISELLE. 12 [?] landed 1.30pm about 130 am Hostile Gun fire directed on our [?] bombardment around MEAULTE. Bath started to be Built from 1.30 am until 2.30 AM. A	
4	Bde HQ started from 2/4 pm. A 5 pm 5am [?] division of MAMETZ WOOD. 1 lines. Attempts made by Hostile hostile to [?] battery. Hun men [?] to reach [?] silent to [?] [?] barrage from enemy.	

10th BATTALION K.O. YORKSHIRE L.I.
WAR DIARY.

DATE AND PLACE.	DETAIL.	REMARKS AND APPENDICES.			
		K.W.	W.	K.	W. Others
Trenches 6	Relieved 6th & 7th Yorks in Left Sub-sector from in of Fricourt. Relief completed 10pm. A quiet night. Others had been sent thirty mins earlier, in view of any possibly treacherous attempt by prisoners.				3
7	[illegible]				1
8	Heavy artillery and trench mortars active. [illegible] Several fruitless attempts to knock out our Q.M.'s. Very heavy bombardment from 11.30pm until 12.30am at night carried out by hostile artillery.				1
9	[illegible]				2
10	Relieved by 6 Som L.I. and Amalgt E BVIGE.				
	Marched to Fricourt into Corps Reserve.				
11	2nd in Command Major G. Jones, Capt F.E. Lask				
12	[illegible] Capt [illegible] in command of Batt. [illegible]				
13	Major B. May, IV B. Stewart [illegible] Major G. Alexander [illegible] Amalgt [illegible] Captain [illegible] [illegible] Berlin.				

10th BATTALION K.O. YORKSHIRE L.I.
WAR DIARY.

DATE AND PLACE.		DETAIL.	REMARKS AND APPENDICES.			
				K.	W.	K. W.
1916						
La NEUVILLE	14	Bath in British Brewery town provided themselves				
	15	"				
	16	Battn. inspected by G.O.C. 64 Bde. Lut. HEYGATE reported				
	17	Inspected Lewis Gunners' equipment				
		Arrived 2/Lt Sinnigan A.A.F. Bomb O. 2/Lt Dixon O.D. P.G. 17/6/15				
		I.G.O. 2/Lt Jack I.L. T.O. 2/Lt Willingham S.C. Gas				
		Lt. Col. Dimech M.C.C.G. and Adjt Asst.				
	18	Route ¾ Guides Lectures				
BELMONT	19	" 2/Lt Smith 2/Lt Herbert S.O.				
		2/Lt Inskip Sharp L.E.				
		Lt. Simpson Shindler ? S.G.				
		2/Lt Woodhouse Smith G Quar. Mr.				
		G.M.H. A. V. S. Buchanan Rifle Asst.				
	20	" Buchanan				
BURY	21	Major C.O. lecs. Orders that Battn. to Bivre.				
	22	Roll Call Battn. Marched Rec. Sev. Coy.				
	23	Lectures				
	24	V. Serg. Distribution of ammunition the Battn. was				
		inspected, lined up. BURY				
	25	Battn. took over Support trenches heavily bombarded on				
		relieved.				

10th BATTALION K.O. YORKSHIRE L.I.
WAR DIARY.

DATE AND PLACE.	DETAIL.	REMARKS AND APPENDICES. K. W. K. W. K. W.
June BURBURE 28	Battn. moved up to Ooremby trenches. Moved off from 9pm (CANCELLED at 2PM) Generall Assy. delayed 48 hrs.	
29	Battn. moved up to Ooremby trenches with new men due tomorrow	
30	ready to chase into outposts of bombardment and discharge of smoke and gas. Enemy Artillery not active	

64th Inf.Bde.
21st Div.

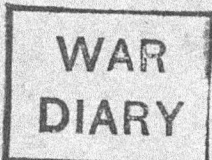

10th BATTN. THE KING'S OWN (YORKSHIRE LIGHT INFANTRY).

J U L Y

1 9 1 6

Attached:

Appendix I.

10th BATTALION K.O. YORKSHIRE L.I.
WAR DIARY.

6/21

DATE AND PLACE		DETAIL.	REMARKS AND APPENDICES.
	July		Officers / Other Ranks
			W / M / K / W / M
TRENCHES	1.	The British offensive commenced. This battalion leading the 64 Brigade assault. They left the trenches at 7·30 a.m. and took CRUCIFIX TRENCH that morning & held it till early the next when they were relieved by the 1st LINCOLNS. Operation Orders Appendix 1.	8 / 9 / 16 / — / 50 / 292 / 135
	2.	Battalion moved to Sausage Support trench, where Major F.S. Lake took command in place of Lt.Col. H.T. KING who had been wounded.	
DERNACOURT	3.	Battalion moved back to DERNACOURT arriving there about midnight, where they bivouacced for the night.	
Ally~~frais~~	4.	The Battalion moved by train to AILLY-sur-SOMME arriving	
LA CHAUSSEE		12·50 pm from where they marched to LA CHAUSSEE arriving 2·30 pm. Resting.	
	5	~~Company Drill Rot~~ LA	
	6	~~Battalion move~~ to MESGE	
MESGE	7·8·9·	Drill & Coy. & Brigade Highland Light Infantry assumed temporary Command of the Battalion.	
On Route to VILLE	10	Battalion marched AILLY-sur-SOMME, thence to CORBIE and from there marched to VILLE. Draft of 30 reinforcements arrived.	
VILLE	11	Battalion arrived at VILLE at 5 a.m. on 11. Draft of 200 reinforcements arrived. Bottom board & Quakeragh Trenches	
VILLE	12.	Battalion moved at 4 p.m. to QUEENS REDOUBT via MEAULTE	

11.11.
8 sheets

10th BATTALION K.O. YORKSHIRE L.I.
WAR DIARY.

DATE AND PLACE		DETAIL.	REMARKS AND APPENDICES. Officers / Other Ranks					
			K	W	M	K	W	M
TRENCHES.	July 13.	Bottom Wood [struck through text]						
	14.	Battalion returned from the to the Bottom Wood [struck through text] relieved by Suffolks to Hade						
	15.	Battalion moved to BAZENTIN village where Lt. AR F SIMPSON was killed. Major LASKIE & Lt. CEWWAIT were wounded.	2	1		3	69	42
	16.	Very heavy shelling. Lt. R.F. WAIT died of wounds. Attack BAZENTIN & PETIT bomb N.W. of hill. Companies [illegible] at [illegible] to support B. 6 C.R. Wood at night						
	17.	Relieved by Suffolk Regt.						
	18.	Battalion Bivouacked in Corps reserve at MEAULTE. Men bivouaced						
MEAULTE	19.	[illegible] MEAULTE						
On route to DREUIL	20.	Battalion marched to MERICOURT STATION trained to SALEUX & marched to DREUIL arriving about 1 am where they bivouaced.						
DREUIL	21.	Resting.						
	22.	Resting.						
On route to HOUVIN	23.	0730am. Battalion marched via AMIENS to LONGUEAU where from where they moved by train to PETIT HOUVIN marching from there to HULLIO at HOUVIN where they arrived 8.45 pm.						
HOUVIN	24, 25, 26, 27.	Reorganising						
	28.	Battalion moved into bivouacs at NOYELLETTE at 4 pm.						
NOYELLETTE	29.	Reorganising etc.						
	30.	The Battalion marched to DOISSANS where they were in Div. Reserve						
	31.	Reorganisation						

B. E. Chilyh Lt. Col.
10/K.O. Yorkshire L.I.
Comg.

A P P E N D I X I.

APPENDIX I.

OPERATION ORDERS 6 BY LIEUT COLONEL KING

Commanding 10th Bn. K.O.Y.L.I.

Map Reference TRENCH MAP.
MONTAUBAN.

Signed by C/O

1. GENERAL ATTACK.

The Battalion will form part of the assaulting line of the 64th Brigade in an attack on the German Position, in which the 21st Division, with the 7th Division on their right and the 34th Division on their left will take part.
The 63rd Brigade will attack on the right of this Brigade.
This Battalion with the 9th K.O.Y.L.I. on their right and the 15th Royal Scots on their left will form part of the first assaulting line and will be supported by 1st E. Yorkshire Regiment. The supporting Battalions on our right being the 15th Durham Light Infantry and on our left the 16th Royal Scots followed by the 27th N.F.

2. OBJECTIVE.

The objective of this Battalion is to sieze the Easterly side SHELTER WOOD, from BIRCH TREE WOOD to X 22 c.5.2. and to consolidate a position in rear thereof, from ROUND WOOD along CRUCIFIX TRENCH ((straddling SUNK ROAD) to X 21. d.8.0.
As soon as SHELTER WOOD is seized word must be sent back and the Supporting Battalion, 1st EAST Yorks, will pass through us and proceed to the second objective which is QUADRANGLE TRENCH.
A Company of R. E. will move forward in rear of this Battalion for the purpose of constructing Strong Points in CRUIFIX TRENCH and SHELTER WOOD.
The various objectives and strong points are marked on map attached hereto.

3. PREPARATION.

The attack will be preceeded by five days bombardment the days being referred to in these orders as V W X Y Z, in the course of which the enemy wire will be cut and trenches destroyed up to and beyond the second objective of the Brigade.
Smoke and Gas will be used if the wind is favorable.

3 A.

During the preliminary bombardment the Battalion will remain in BUIRE and move to the assembly trenches on the night of X/Y and will be responsible for cutting the wire on our Battalion front. O.C. of the Compan--ies leading in the assault will be responsible for the proper cutting of the wire.

3 B.

At an hour to be given later the Battalion will move to the Assembly trenches and will take up positions in Assembly Trenches as shown on tracing attached hereto.
Battalion Headquarters in dug-out at head of ABOYNE STREET.
Regimental Aid Post reinforced by 10 R.A.M.C. bearers in ABERDEEN AVENUE near DINET CUT.
Reserve S.A.A. and Bombs with Battalion Head--quarters.

4. ASSAULT.

The assault of this Battalion will be made in depth with two Companies in front and two Companies in support.
Each Company will attack on a front of One Platoon. Each platoon will be extended to cover its allotted front.
"B" Company will form the assaulting Company

(Company) .2.

4. ASSAULT.
(Continued)

on the right and "A" Company on the left, being supported respectively by "B" and "C" Companies.
All ranks must understand the extreme importance of maintaining direction.

4. A.

The attack will be launched at ZERO on Zero Day and will be proceeded by an intense bombardment.

A+B. Companies

A five minutes before Zero the first and second Platoons of assaulting Companies will leave our front line trenches and crawl forward as close to the German front line as our barrage will permit. Directly our barrage lifts the first and second platoons will cross the German front line trench and continue their advance to the first objective. at 50 yds distance
Remaining platoons will follow at a distance of not more than one hundred yards.

C+D Companies

Officer Commanding "C" Coy. and "D" Coy. will detail their leading platoons as clearing parties and will have them follow closely in the rear of the fourth platoon of the assaulting Companies.

Bombers

Officer Commanding Bombers will attach to "A" Coy. four squads to act as blocking parties for KIPPER TRENCH, SANDWICH TRENCH, WHISKY TRENCH, WOOD ALLEY. These blocking parties will move forward with the second and fourth waves on the left of "A" Coy. Blocking parties on the arrival of the Division on our left will immediately rejoin "A" Company and will be at the disposal of O.C. "A" Coy. for futher blocking or as a reinforcement for defensive measures.

? Withdrawn of Green Redoubt

x

The Platoon bombing squads of the third and fourth platoons of "C" and "D" Companies will be attached to the clearing platoons. Clearing parties will carry forward two Vermoral Sprayers per platoon together with all available electric torches for use while clearing out dug-outs. Every dug-out must be searched as quickly as possible. This party must be prepared to render assistance to clearing parties adjacent to them or to blocking parties if necessary. But unless absolutely necessary they will not leave the work assigned to them.
On finishing their work they will rejoin their Companies

? attack will be before ours

4. B.

Owing to the attack on our left not being timed simultaneously with ours, the left flank Companies must take special precautions for protection of their left flank.
Great care must be taken by all Company and Platoon Commanders to keep in touch with the Battalons attacking on our right and left.

4. C.

Trench Mortar Battery support will be given to the assaulting by opening fire on the German lines simultaneously with the attack. This fire will cease immediately the Infantry are within 50 yards of the German Trenches.

5. SIGNALS.

Each Company will have attached to them 6 Signallers as well as 8 Runners; Bombing Officer will have one Signaller attached to him. Battalion Headquarters will have 20 Signallers attached. Immediately after the four waves of the Assaulting Companies have gone forward, Linesmen will commence laying a wire to new Headquarters in DINGLE TRENCH. This will be run forward between the two Companies so that in an emergency it can be made use of. Signalling Officer will also be responsible for the keeping of communi--cation with Brigade Headquarters.

.3.

BARRAGE.
Artillery barrage will be carried out according to definite programme and a proposed schedule of the time on which the barrage will lift to a given line will be issued to all ranks Officers and N.C.O's.

IT IS TO BE REMEMBERED however, that this barrage will be lifted gradually, sweeping the entire ground before it, and the troops must move forward as it advances so as to take all advantages of its protection.

As unforeseen circumstances may cause an alteration in the times of lifting the barrage the Infantry should follow, by creeping if necessary, the line of the burst of shells as closely as possible. (Shrapnell always bursts forward). All the guns of the Trench Mortar Battery will fire during the last four minutes of the bombardment.

7. STRONG POINTS.
The Battalion must consolidate at every pause in the advance by digging in or reversing hostile trenches but will not stop their forward movement unnecessarily to do this. The value of the trenching tool must not be forgotten. Strong Points will be garrisoned by this Battalion as marked on map attached. These points will be prepared by the engineers and Company Officers are responsible that covering parties are formed to protect them against counter attack.

8. EQUIPMENT.
In the attack the Battalion will wear skeleton equipment with waterproof cases rolled on the belt in the rear. Each man will carry 220 rounds S.A.A and 2 Mills Grenades in his pocket. Each man will leave the trenches with water bottle filled, the unexpired portion of the days rations and his emergency rations; one tin in 4 will be opened at a time, providing four meals.

Bombs carried by the men will be collected at the first objective to form a Bomb store for each Coy.

The three rear platoons of the supporting Companies will detail parties to carry forward 20 boxes S.A.A. which will be slung in bandoliers across 20 men.

Supporting Companies will be responsible for the following carrying:-
Excepting the trench clearing platoons each man will carry either a pick or a shovel.
Twenty boxes of S.A.A.
Forty large buckets of Mills Grenades.
The latter will be drawn from the Assembly trenches.

9. HEADQUARTERS.
Commanding Officer and Hdqrs. will move forward to the DINGLE as a wave immediately in front of the last two lines, one half the Bombing Platoon on the left of the line, and the runners, signallers on the left and centre respectively.

All undirected ammunition carriers will take surplus ammunition and Bombs to this point so as to form a forward ammunition Depot.

10. MEDICAL.
The Regimental Aid Post will remain at ABERDEEN Av. until the first objective is reached when it will move forward and take up a position in the DINGLE near new Battalion Headquarters.

Stretcher bearers will accompany their Companies and will render such First Aid as they can before taking back stretcher cases. Slightly wounded men will carry on with the Battalion unless they are detailed to escort prisoners.

.4.

11. TRANSPORT. A Echelon Transport will park in a selected position near VILLE and will come under the orders of the STAFF Captain 64th Brigade. Messages for same will be sent to Staff Captain to OLD BRIGADE HEADQUARTERS, MEAULTE.

12. REPORTS. The situation to be reported to the Headquarters at least every hour.
All ranks will be supplied with flares for use with Aeroplane, and these will be used to show the position reached at

9.A.M.   1.P.M.   5.P.M.   9.P.M.

Flags will be supplied to the left flank Company to be shown, for the direction of the Brigade on our left, who will also act in a similar manner.

13. CONTROL POSTS. THE Battalion will detail ~~from their Police~~ POLICE one N.C.O. and four men for control of the Up and Down trenches in the Brigade Assembly Area.
Up trenches DINNET ST.
Continuation of DINNET St. into the German front line.
These Control Posts will be formed up in the Assembly Trenches on the night of Y/Z and will remain on duty until the arrival of the 62nd Brigade, when they will rejoin their Battalion.

14. MISCELLANEOUS. The following additional points are to be brought to the notice of all ranks.

(1) All ranks must know the time and positions of the successive barrages. The success of the operations will depend largely upon the troops following up the barrages as closely as possible

(2) In case of emergency Commanding Officers will call upon the nearest Machine Gun for assistance
Two Stokes guns will move forward in rear of the Supporting Companies of the assulting Battalion and will be at the disposal of the Commanding Officer of the Battalion.

(3) The word RETIRE is not to be used under any circumstances and no man will be justified in letting go a forward position once he has obtained same.

(4) Except in cases of extreme emergency only men trained as bombers will throw MILLS Grenades.
Every effort is to be made to avoid wasting these bombs by throwing them into empty fire bays or dugouts.

(5) On no account are the coloured Artillery boards to be moved from German Trenches. The removal of these boards is a signal to German Artillery that the trench is in our hands.

(3) Full use must be made of all German bombs, tools and wire. A systematic search should be made for these stores after capturing each trench.

(4) Each successive wave passing over the German trenches should be on the look-out for Germans getting up to fire from their trenches into the backs of the men in front.
Men should be ready to shoot down into each

.5.

Trench as they reach it if necessary.

15. TIME.   All Time in connection with these orders will be reckoned from Zero.
At the time when all watches in the Battalion are synchronizised the actual hour of ZERO will be notified.

Lieut. Colonel.
Commanding, 10th Bn. K. O. Y. L. I.

? drawing bombs.
S.A.A:
Tools for Supporting Coys.
Where to draw them etc.
Flags for marking line of Advance

64th Brigade.

21st Division.

10th BATTALION

KING's OWN YORKSHIRE LIGHT INFANTRY

AUGUST 1916

10th BATTALION K.O. YORKSHIRE L.I.
WAR DIARY.

DATE AND PLACE		DETAIL.	REMARKS AND APPENDICES.
DUISANS	1	Rest	
"	2	Rest	
"	3	Rest	
"	4	Battalion moved to trenches at ARRAS. at 8 pm to relieve 15th Bn Durham L.Infty	
"	5	Relief completed by 1.30 am	
"	6	Quiet	
"	7	"	
"	8	"	
"	9	"	
"	10	Relieved by 15th Bn Durham L.I. Commencing at 10 p.m Completed by 12 P.M.	
BRIGADE RESERVE	11	Battalion was distributed as follows: A & B Coy's 15th Bays at ARRAS. 1 Coy at ROCKLINGCOURT 1 Coy at ST. NICHOLAS Working Parties	
"	12	"	
"	13	"	
"	14	3rd f.d. Amm. joined Bn from Cadet School.	
"	15	"	
"	16	Battalion relieved 15th Bn Durham L.I. in trenches commencing 2 pm completed by 6 pm	
"	17	Quiet	
"	18	2 Lieuts H.M. Even & S.O. Dexter joined Bn from Base Depot. 3rd f.d. Amm. rejoined	
"	19	3 Privates joined Bn from Base Depot	
"	20		

10th BATTALION K.O. YORKSHIRE L.I.
WAR DIARY.

DATE AND PLACE		DETAIL.	REMARKS AND APPENDICES.
Junchee	August 21	Quiet	
	22	Relieved by 15 Bn Durham L.I. completed by 6.30 pm & then marched to DUISANS	
DUISANS	23	Spare for 6 Inst.	
	24	" " "	
	25	" " "	
	26	" " "	
	27	" " "	
	28	Relieved 15th Durham L.I. in trenches leaving DUISANS at 8 & relief completed at 1.30 a.m. (29)	
	29	Quiet. Capt T.G. Clarke joins Bn from Base Depot	
	30	Rather a bombardment with trench mortars. 16 Germans raided our front line trench leaving behind two a large quantity of hand grenades & at least three 6 kilo jam tins Shell	
Junchee	31	Quiet	

[signatures]

1.9.16

Lieut Colonel
Comdg 10 Bn (S) K.O. Yorks L.I.

64th Brigade
21st Division.

10th BATTALION

KING'S OWN YORKSHIRE LIGHT INFANTRY

SEPTEMBER 1916

10th BATTALION K.O. YORKSHIRE L.I.
WAR DIARY.

DATE AND PLACE.		DETAIL.	REMARKS AND APPENDICES.
Juncheux	2	Quiet	
"	3	"	
"	4	Bns relieved by 8th Locals. Completed Bn left and then marched to L'AGNEZ-LES-DUISANS (DIVISIONAL RELIEF). Guides in billets by 6pm. Bn sent forward from Dunlam & Bathis joined Bn.	
"	5	Marched off at 8am to IZEL-LES-HAMEAU for rest & training. Compatible billets by 1pm.	
AGNEZ-LES-DUISANS IZEL-LE-HAMEAU	6	Bathing. Resting. Training up. 199 (Reinforcements) joined Bn. Some found.	
"	7	Training continued. 5 N.F.s & 41 LINCOLNS. REGT. transferred to this unit.	
"	8	Training. Reinforcements 30 Joined (York. Som found)	
"	9	Training	
"	10	3 1/2 B.B. Billy. Bn paraded 8.0.0 looks 6 mill attendance joined from Cadets School, 3/h transferred to Hospital	
"	11	8.0am marched to HOUVIN-HOUVIGNEUL at 2.15pm. Received Billets for the night	
HOUVIN-HOUVIGNEUL FREVENT	12	8.0am marched to FREVENT STATION at 13. Bn entrained at 11.30am. Detrained at PERICOURT Stn at 12 noon. Marched to L'DERNACOURT. Bath arrived Bull-in by 3 pm. Reinforcement 14 (Offy 24) arrived. MAJOR C.A. Holland Joined.	
DERNACOURT	14	Resting	
"	15	8.0Ahrs left base for FRICOURT CAMP then after resting marched to POMIERES REDOUBT. Awaiting orders.	
POMIERES REDOUBT	16	Marched to SWITCH TRENCH at 1.30am in close order. By 15.0AM tat 9.30am. No attacks were found. Bns went through barrage (enemy) from 3/6 High-line Shrdler Valley (wounded) those shown in Colours attached were unsuccessful. Heavily bombarded by enemy artillery.	1 3 1 8 29 18

10th BATTALION K.O. YORKSHIRE L.I.
WAR DIARY.

DATE AND PLACE.		DETAIL.	REMARKS AND APPENDICES.			
				Officers	Other ranks	
				K	W	K	W
FLERS TRENCH	17	Gentle artillery bombardment of our trenches by enemy which lasted practically all day. Suffering by following casualties. 2/Lt Gristhorpe (wounded) at night we were relieved by 5 Bn. King's Liverpool Regt. relief complete by 9.30 pm & thus marched to POMIERES REDOUBT, arriving there at 3 am		1	2	
POMIERES REDOUBT	18	After picking pans to FRICOURT CAMP at 11am				
FRICOURT CAMP	19	During it ASHBY RMC Lt. R.A.F. for us to 3rd Anti. Clearing Station. 2/Lt L.O. Jones for hospital & ord.				1st Oct 1
	20	Resting				
	21					
	22	Bn marches to trenches N of BERNAFAY WOOD & was in Brig. Reserve 6/7 days. Capt Elghove joined from 9 Regt L				
BERNAFAY WOOD	23	Bn marches to trenches. Relieved 12th N.F. Relief completed by 12 midnight				
FLERS	24	Trenches quiet				
	25	At 12.35pm heavy [?] bombardment by enemy & the following casualties [?] Blackburn missing				1st Oct 1
		Bn attacked FLERS & of GOUDECOURT under heavy barrage of artillery fire, was very successful. Roe very severe. Bn was held up. Casualties:- Killed 2/Lts Bartolozzi L, Kenbooro 2/Lts Huntworth				
		Halt of Gaughey, Knowles attacking Newbold 2/Lts Dixon Dow, Topacslaw, Graham, Ritchie				413 1189 99
		Gharley, Allen, [?]				1 1 1
GOUDECOURT	26	Enemy in retreat Bn advanced Thorn Hook up on outward line about 1600 then escorted [?] Crest				
		at night relieved then marches to BERNAFAY WOOD				
BERNAFAY WOOD	27	Resting & cleaning up				
	28	Bn marches to POMIERES REDOUBT. J [?] here				
	29	Bn marches to RIBEMONT. Training & reinforcements 50 NC [?]				
RIBEMONT	30	for the details				
		1.10.16				

B.L. Bright, Lieut Colonel
Commanding 10 Bn. the K.O. Yorkshire L.I.

Major C.A. Milward, Indian Army.
G.S.O.2, 20th (Light) Division.
Vol. IV.   1916.
To 10th K.O.Y.L.I., as 2nd in command

25th September 1916.

I went all round the trenches early in the morning mist, and saw all the companies ready for the attack settled in the Assembly Trenches, some of which had only been dug during the night.

All seemed quite ready, complete with food and water (about which I had taken great trouble) ammunition, bombs, S.O.S. Rockets, signal flares, Very pistols and cartridges, and orders and plan of attack, including compass bearings of advance.

At 11:30 am. I was sent back half-an-hour's walk to Brigade Hqrs. to help there, and to preserve my precious life to await my C.O's being made a casualty, when I was to go up to take his place. Two other officers were sent back to the Transport.

Our artillery bombardment had been going on since 7 am. yesterday - shrapnel 18 pr. and Heavy Artillery. The noise had been deafening, and the village and enemy's trenches were in a cloud of dust.

The Zero hour was 12:35 when the Infantry attack began, and the Artillery fire became intense. The Brigade Hqrs. was situated in a crowded dug-out for 2 Brigades, in the middle of the line of guns. The noise was awful, but it made one feel proud to see what our munition workers and Great Britian had been able to accomplish.

The 18-pounder Field Artillery Shrapnel Barrage was to creep forward 50 yards a minute, close under which the assaulting infantry were to advance.

We were to take the first objective, another battalion coming up from behind to make the second objective, after 1 hour's halt for consolidation, and mopping up of dug-outs with smoke bombs. Then after another hour - at 2:35 pm. we were to advance to the third objective.

The idea is to advance so close under the Artillery Barrage that we get there before the enemy (taking shelter in his dug-outs) has time to emerge, when he is met at the top of the stairs by our men and dealt with.

All reports were good at first. We had taken the first objective, and the Brigades on our right and left hand had done ditto. Certainly the Guards on the right had done so, as they always would; but the report that the Leicester Brigade on the left had taken Gueudecourt was not true.

The Germans with signal flares similar to our euw own had misled our aircraft. We were wupposed to be settled in gird support trench, but this was not so.

The Battalions coming up from behind to take the second objective had been able to get through the enemy's Barrage only after such heavy casualties that it had been unable to proceed.

In fact, about 3 pm. the situation was so obscure that the G.O.C. (Headlam) told me to go up to Colonel Bridge at Battn. Hqrs., Sunken Road, to clear it all up.

It was a half-hour's wlak through the trenches. and I expected to have to pass through the enemy's Barrage, but except for a few shells, he had shifted it.

The communication trenches were much blocked with wounded. Two Regiments of Cavalry, of the Indian Cavalry Division,※

※ 6th Dragoons and 19th Bengal Lancers.

---

had now moved up to Brigade Headqrs., ready to break through.

On arrival I found Bridges, who stated that he believed his men had moved right on to the 3rd objective when the supporting Battalion had not arrived according to schedule. All his runners with messages had been shot, and he was cut off.

One of the reasons for my despatch to see Colonel Bridges

was the aeroplane report that the front German trench (Gird Trench) was full of Germans, packed, who had evidently worked their way behind our men in Gird support Trench, working down from the village. Colonel Bridges was nervous for the safety of his own original front line, and so I went down and along it to find out how things stood.

I found the trench full of dead and wounded, and full of a mixture of men - men of the two supporting battalions who had reached it after passing through the enemy's Barrage - the 9th K.O.Y.L.I. and 1st Lincolns. They had lost heavily, had few officers left, and no organisation - no sentries - all mixed up.

They did not realise they had the enemy in front of them.

I got them organised and sorted out, and sentries posted, and returned to Battn Headquarters.

I was just on my way back to report to the G.O.C., when a message came in at last from our front line. It reported that our men had never entered the German front line. They had found the enemy's wire uncut and very thick, it was in a hallow and could not be seen, and they had been met with machine-gun fire. They had all (4 coys) lain down in shell holes in front of the enemy's wire, waiting for the darkness. In the advance, their casualties had been slight. I now returned over the two miles of desolate shell holes and trenches to Brigade Headquarters to report.

The situation at 7 pm. was that the troops on our right had got on to their third objective, those on the left had reached their first objective, but not the village - and we had got nowhere with supports and Reserves in no state to advance - not a military body.

Division ordered immediate resumption of attack, but this was impossible with wire still uncut.

Suggestions of bombing attack from the South, use of "Tanks" (Caterpillars) were discussed.

The only thing that was done was the collection during the night of our men from in front of the wire - but their

casualties had now been heavy. They had been killed by enemy
machine-guns in the open, bombed in the shell-holes, and caught
again as they retired to our line. I was sent back to help
the C.O., arriving about 10 pm. in the Sunken Road.

The Sunken Road was in an awful state of congestion - full
of wounded and stretchers and blocked with men. The dressing
station was crammed and the Doctor working like a hero. The
enemy were shelling the road and as we sat there burst a
shrapnel over our heads, a bullet of which bounced off a man's
stell helmet with a bang. A weak Battalion was arriving to take
over our original front line - the mixture of supporting
Battalions there being withdrawn.

We had an appalling night in our dug-out, more crowded than
ever and little sleep.

26th September 1916.

By morning the remnants of our Battalion had been collected
in the support trench close to Battalion Headquarters.

We were having our breakfast (little of it) in the end of
the trench, when looking towards Gueudecourt I noticed thick
white smoke travelling along in front of it - a "Tank".

Twenty minutes later the Asjutant got excited and we ran
up to the captured German guns on the bank of the Sunken Road,
and saw streams of Germans coming across No Man's Land to
surrender. They came across and up the Sunken Road, headed by
their Battalion Commander -a coarse looking brute, with his
servant carrying a hand-bag. He explained that his Battalion had
been holding Gird Trench. His right and left had been cut by the
advance of our right and left Brigades yesterday.

He had no communication trenches, and suddenly the
appearance in his rear of a tank had completed his envelopment
and he had to surrender.

On and on they came in streams - 362 were counted. We
collected all the officer's papers. Colonel Bridges got a
first-class pair of field glasses, and I collected 50 of them and
sent them back to collect and carry in our wounded under escort,
and all were despatched to the rear. We now had to push forward

to our original front line while the troops then occupied Gird Trench and beyond. All was now rosy - the Brigade on the left pushed on patrols to find out if the village was occupied.

About 12 noon we received orders to push forward a line of posts to the original 3rd objective - the village was empty (so they said) with our left on the village - the 15th D.L.I. on our right.

We collected for this in the front line - such as were left of us - not many. But the enemy spotted the movement and started shelling with 8 inch H.E. And a very bad time he gave us. Colonel Bridges was trying to talk to the General on the telephone - I at his elbow - half in a trench. Three shells, out of the many which arrived, came over quite close and covered up with lumps of earth, but the conversation went on as far as possible in the noise.

My batman - Morton - broke down and howled like a babe, and was about to beat a retreat when I ordered him back to his hole We were in a sunken road.

Further we heard from the 'Tank' man who had returned, covered with blood and bound up, that he had crawled his Tank over the village and instead of meeting 50 Germans as expected he had come across 500 whom he had taken on. In the end he had out of petrol, but had managed to get back himself. Consequently our advance was postponed.

Eventually, about 3 pm, we advanced cautiously to Gird Trench saw the wire uncut and our men lying in front. It was pleasant, however, to walk into an empty German trench and to explore.

I was sent to get in touch with the Battalion on our right. The enemy had retired a long way, and our men were in the village, or in most of it. There were, however, a lot of long-range machine-gun bullets from the further ridge flying about one's ankles, and shells too. We had pushed on our Posts to ta up their line and our supports too. Battalion Headquarters, too, advanced behind them, and saw them settled in some shell-holes. They were immediately spotted and had a shell very close. I left them there to visit the front line of posts and supports. I

6.

found the latter digging in - the going was not pleasant, bullets and shell holes - one wounded German Officer who waved to me hard but no time to visit him, and would'nt trust him.

As I got nearer the village of Gueudecourt on my left in the hollw, one became more and more exposed moving down the forward slope of our plateau, and in face of the big slope and ridge opposite, which was held by the Germans whom one could see running along the skyline.

They had attempted a counter attack in the village, but had been dispersed by our Artillery, and the Lewis guns of our Posts and had retired up the slope and over. Two cavalry regts. had now entered the village but could not get on.

I found Posts in shell holes, of Leicesters, but none of our own, who had edged over to the left and joined the next Battalion in the village. I thought I would push on and called to my orderly, "Come on". To my disgust the inhabitants of all the shell-holes around (about 30) answered my call and came. We drew a lot of accurate long range Machine-gun fire so we all retired again into shell-holes for the time being. Unfortunately the German Artillery, too, had spotted them or me, and opened an intense fire for a time.

At my hole they made some very good shooting, putting two Whiz-Bangs within 3-5 yards of me. My orderly and I cowered low in our tiny hole.

The view was fine and most interesting. As soon as it was dark we wandered around and found our people. Then returned. We were to be relieved at night.

I thought the Colonel would be anxious about me but on my wat back I heard him hollering and found him marching the Headqrs. Party forward. The enemy had detected them back in their shell-holes and given them an awful time with 5.9 and 8-inch. Among oht other things they had spattered the beef for dinner all over with earth and made it uneatable. They did'nt seem a bit anxious about me.

They were on their way to a good dug-out which had been discovered in a second Sunken Road near the original second objective. As we approached, the enemy were shelling the road and the derelict Tank.

I suggested that it would be better perhaps to get down the dug-out instead of standing in a crowd of about 15 at its mouth, and led the way. I got eto the bottom of the steps, Colonel B Bridges was at the top, and I was thinking how one shell down the steps would bag us both, when "bang" out went the candle and there was a roar up above. A shell had hit the sunken road bank just above, knocked over the Artillery Officer, and slightly wounded another and a man.

The dug-out was filthy, full of paper and stuff, but it had two rooms whose floors were large mattresses.

We had quite a good dinner and then I went sound asleep on the mattress for 2 hours. On awaking I found there was a mix-up about the Reliefs. I had to take one party out about 2 am. to find and relieve our support Company. It was most difficult to find them in the pitch dark and the open trackless country, covered with huge shell holes with occasional shells about, but we did it in the end, and about 3 am. we started off on our crawl homewards past old Battn Hqrs. up the Sunken Road, past old Bde H.Q. back 3 miles to the wagon lines. We reached here at 7 am. 27th., with 5 days8 beard and filthy, our feet very sore from continually wearing our boots.

Lieut Colonel C.A.Milward to 9/K.O.Y.L.I. also 21st Division, as C.O. back to Indian Army March 1917.

Vol 74

War Diary
of
10th KO's L.I.
for
month of October /16.

10th BATTALION K.O. YORKSHIRE L.I.
WAR DIARY.

DATE AND PLACE	1916 Oct.	DETAIL.	REMARKS AND APPENDICES.
RIBEMONT	1	Resting	
"	2	"	
"	3	Entrained to MERICOURT. Entrained from there to LONGPRE at 12 noon arrived LONGPRE 4/30pm. Marched to BELLANCOURT arriving in billets at 10.15pm.	
BELLANCOURT	4	Resting. Major E.A. Meinour transferred to 9KOYLI as Infantry in Command	
"	5	2/Lt. G.D. Jones & F.H. Benefield transferred to 15/DLI as 2/Lt. 2/Lt. A.B. BARRETT appointed a/Adjutant. 5 O.R. Joined	
"	6	Capt. E.P. CLARKE transferred to 9KOYLI.	
"	7	Capt. M. Rev. J. REDMOND joined Batt. as Chaplain C/E	
"	7	Batt. marched to ABBEVILLE and entrained at 8.30pm for CHOCQUES. Arrived 7am marched to billets at ALLOUAGNE.	
ALLOUAGNE	8	MAJOR F.I.M. POSTLETHWAITE returns & takes on Strength. Capt. R.H. HINE HAYCOCK.	
"	9	Following joined & taken on Strength. Capt. R.H. HINE HAYCOCK. Lt. C.D. JONES; 2/Lt C.W. BUSKIN.	
"	10	Following joined at 2--9p.m. R.T. JAMES, G.A. BRIERLEY, A. FOX, H.N. ATTWELL, T.B. LITTLE (J.P.), H.T. HOLDSTOCK, J.P. SHAW, H.A. LE FEUVRE, E.B. YARDLEY, R.M. COUPLAND, V. WISEMAN, L.J.L. WAY, B. COOPER, J.T. JONES, V.M. BELL	
BETHUNE	11	Batt. marched to BETHUNE & went into billets.	
TRENCHES (B CAMBRIN SECTOR)	12	Relieves 1/9 HLI at 6PM.	16 1

10th BATTALION K.O. YORKSHIRE L.I.
WAR DIARY.

DATE AND PLACE		DETAIL.	REMARKS AND APPENDICES.			
1916	Oct.		Officers		Other Ranks	
			K. W. M.		K. W. M.
"	14.	Transport & QM Stores established at BEUVRY.				
"	15.	Lt. J. SHEFFIELD joined. 16/10/16. 2/Lt PT. LISTER to 9/KOYLI; 2 OR joins				1
"	17.	Following transferred to 9/KOYLI:— Lt. COTONES, 2/Lts G.T. INKPEN,	17/10/16			
"		C.Q. GREENLEY, T.R. LITTLE, J.C. SHAW, J.L. WAY.				
SUPPORT TRENCHES	18.	Batt: moved into VILLAGE LINE in support.				
"		2/Lt. HERBERT appointed Town Major ANNEQUIN.				
"	19.	2/Lt. WALBY joined. 21/10/16. 2/Lt. INGPEN rejoined from 9th Batt.				
L. CAMBRIN SECTOR	24.	Batt: moved into front line L. CAMBRIN SECTOR, relieving	25/10/16			1
"		151st D.L.I.				
ANNEQUIN.	27.	Batt: moved into rest in BDE RESERVE.				
"	28.	Baths for all ranks. 29.10.16 2 OR joins				
"	30.	2 OR joins. LIEUT. H. BURKETT rejoined.				
"	31.					

J.H. Pettlewood
Major.
Comm. 10th Batt. K.O. Yorkshire Light Infantry.

CONFIDENTIAL

Vol 15

WAR DIARY
— OF —
10TH BN. K.O.Y.L.I.

from 1st Nov. to 30th Nov/16

Army Form C. 2118.

WAR DIARY
or
INTELLIGENCE SUMMARY.
(Erase heading not required.)

NOVEMBER 1916.

Instructions regarding War Diaries and Intelligence Summaries are contained in F. S. Regs., Part II. and the Staff Manual respectively. Title pages will be prepared in manuscript.

Place	Date	Hour	Summary of Events and Information	Remarks and references to Appendices
				Officers / O.R.
				K / W / M / K / W / M
ANNEQUIN	Nov 1		Batt. in Brigade Reserve at ANNEQUIN. 2/Lt J Jones transferred to base.	
TRENCHES	2		Relieved 15/D.L.I in front line. L CAMBRIAN SECTOR.	- 1 2 - - -
	6		13 O.R. joined	- 1 2 - - -
VILLAGE LINE	8		Relieved by 15/D.L.I. & took over VILLAGE LINE in support.	- 1 1 - - - 5/11/16
			2/Lt HERBERT approaches draft conducting officer - struck off strength	- - 2 - - - 6/11/16
	9		2/Lt Gt INKPEN " " " "	- - 1 - - - 13/11/16
TRENCHES	12		Relieved 15/D.L.I in front line. 15.11.16. 208 joined from 32/I.S.D ANNEQUIN	- - 1 - - - 13/11/16
ANNEQUIN	16		Relieved by 15/D.L.I & went into Brigade Reserve at ANNEQUIN.	- - 1 - - - 21/11/16
	17		7 O.R. joined.	- - - - - - 22/11/16
TRENCHES	20		Relieved 15/D.L.I in front line. 22. Nov. 4 O.R. joined.	
VILLAGE LINE	24		Relieved by 15/D.L.I and went into support in VILLAGE LINE	
	29		Relieved in VILLAGE LINE by 11/ESSEX Regt (6th Division) & marches	
			to billets. H.Q. have J/M & D Coys at LA BOURSE: B Coy & remainder	
			of A Coy at SAILLY LA BOURSE: C Coy & remainder of A Coy at NOEUX LES MINES	
LA BOURSE	30		au bonjour nothing	

J.M. Jones
N.C. Bailey
W.G.
Commdt 19 Royal H.

Confidential.

Vol 16

G.D. 16.M.
2 sheets

10th Bn. K.O.Y.L.I.

War Diary for December, 1916.

Army Form C. 2118.

10TH (S) BATTALION.
K.O.Y.L.I.
No. XIV
Date ....

WAR DIARY
or
INTELLIGENCE SUMMARY.
(Erase heading not required.)

Instructions regarding War Diaries and Intelligence Summaries are contained in F.S. Regs., Part II. and the Staff Manual respectively. Title pages will be prepared in manuscript.

Place	Date	Hour	Summary of Events and Information	Remarks and references to Appendices
In Rest	Dec. 1		H.Q. at LABOURSE; "A"&"B" coys at SHILLY LABOURSE; "C"&"D" coys at NOEUX-LES-MINES.	
	2.		9 Sgts joined from 32nd I.B.D.; 80 O.R. from 27th I.B.D.	
			Lt. KEATERIDGE W.R.C. was 20 miles to hospital sick	4/12/16 — 1
	6.		6 O.R. joined from 32 I.B.D. Capt. FRANKLIN re-joined from 21st Div. Bombing School.	
BETHUNE	7.		Batt. marched to BETHUNE & went into billets at MONTMORENCY BARRACKS.	
	8.		Approaches to GIVENCHY SECTOR reconnoitred by Co. & Coy Officers.	
	12.		HOHENZOLLERN Left Subsector reconnoitred by Co. & Coy Officers.	
	14.		12 O.R. joined from 32. I.B.D.	
TRENCHES	15.		"B" moved into HOHENZOLLERN Left Subsector relieving 5/6 Leicesters.	
	16.		Following Officers joined 2/Lieut A.J.PERRIN. H.E.SHARP. W.R.WILKINSON. E.FIRTH. F.S.ELLIS. A.W.NORRIS.	18/12/16 — 1, 2
	19.		3 O.R. joined from. 32? I.B.D.	19/12/16 — 1, 1
	22.		Batt. relieved by 15 D.L.I. & went into Reserve. H.Q.M. & "D" coy LANCASHIRE TRENCH "A" coy	21/12/16 — 1, 1
RESERVE			& "B"&"C" in MAZINGARBE	
	25.		H.O.R. joined from 28/I.B.D.	
	27.		Gun positions behind LANCASHIRE TRENCH shelled chiefly with gas shells, lachrymatory &	
			& Type 85 gun shell bursting with a small detonation, some of these fell in	
			LANCASHIRE TRENCH when "D" coy were in.	
FOUQUEREUIL	28.		Batt. relieved by 2/Bedford Regt. & marched to FOUQUEREUIL billets for training.	
	31.		65 O.R. joined from 32./I.B.D.	

	Officers				Other Ranks			
	K	W	M		K	W	M	
TOTAL					3	4	—	

W.W. Pattullo
Major.
Comdg. 10. K.O.Y.L.I.

Instructions regarding War Diaries and Intelligence Summaries are contained in F. S. Regs., Part II. and the Staff Manual respectively. Title pages will be prepared in manuscript.

WAR DIARY
or
INTELLIGENCE SUMMARY.
(Erase heading not required.)

Army Form C. 2118.

64/31

10 Bn K.O.Y.L.I.

267

Place	Date	Hour	Summary of Events and Information	Remarks and references to Appendices
MOUFREUIL	Jan 1st 1917		Coy. training commenced. Reinforcements. 116 O.R. joined from 32nd I.B.D. not fired Part III musketry	
	2nd		Coy training continued. 21 O.R. joined from 32nd I.B. Depot.	
	3rd		3 O.R. joined from 32nd I.B.D.	
	4th–6th		Coy. training.	
	7th		33 O.R. joined from 32nd I.B.D.	
	8th		2nd Lieut J.A. Hinchcliffe joined from England. 2nd Lieut J.E. Crinkall joined from 32nd I.B.D. 108 O.R. joined from 32 I.B.D.	
	9th		Coy. training.	
	10th		Capt Paton. RAMC returned from leave & transferred to 63rd Field Ambulance.	
	11th		Training.	
	12th		Training. 120 O.R. joined from 32nd I.B.D.	
	13th & 14th		Training. 2nd Lieut Firth admitted to Hospital. 27 O.R. joined from 32nd I.B.D.	
	15th–19th		Training.	
	20th		Bde Horse Show. 1st Prize Officers Chargers 3rd Pack animals. Major H.R. Daniells 9th K.O.Y.L.I. assumed command of the Battn. during Lt Col. Postlethwaite's absence on leave.	
	21st		Lt Col Postlethwaite proceeded on leave. 2nd Lieut R.H. Draper joined from 32nd I.B. Depot. 150 O.R. proceeded to [illegible] for a musketry course. 2nd Lieut Sharp, 2nd Lieut Crinkall & 2nd Lieut [illegible] went with the party	

2353 Wt. W2544/1454 700,000 5/15 D. D. & L. A.D.S.S./Forms/C. 2118.

17.11 2 sheets

Army Form C. 2118.

WAR DIARY
or
INTELLIGENCE SUMMARY.

(Erase heading not required)

Place	Date	Hour	Summary of Events and Information	Remarks and references to Appendices
ROUEN	Jan 22		Lieut C Mitton + Lieut R J Masters posted from 3rd I.B.D.	
	23rd		[illegible] on [illegible] inspection	
	24		3 New P.B. Men reposted from England. Bn marched to Pace.	
	25		C.O., Adj. [illegible], G.M. inter [illegible] [illegible]	
	26		B.O. marched forward of 43rd Inf Bde [illegible]	
	27	5 pm	[illegible]	
	28		[illegible]	
	29		Bn reached FOUQUEREUIL. [illegible] [illegible] 12mm marched forward to WERNYHOUST	
	30		Coy Training.	
WERNYHOUST	31			

[signatures]

WAR DIARY
or
INTELLIGENCE SUMMARY.

(Erase heading not required.)

Army Form C. 2118.

10 K.O.Y.L.I. Vol 18

Place	Date	Hour	Summary of Events and Information	Remarks and references to Appendices
WORMHOUDT.	February 1st		Company training.	
	2nd		do — Lt.Col. POSTLETHWAITE returned from leave.	
	3rd		do — Party of 100 NCOs & men proceeded to TILQUES to fire musketry. Army Commander inspected boys at training.	
	4th		Bde Route march. 2/Lt. G.H. WRAY rejoined. 2/Lt. J.G. HURST reported. 2/Lt. E.H. FIRTH from hospital.	
			4 O.R. from 32nd I.B.D. joined.	
	5th		Work parties — 7 platoons 40 O.R. working on Railways - PROVEN. Major N.R. DANIELLS returned to 9th Bn. K.O.Y.L.I.	
	6th-8th		Work parties & Coy training continued. 8th 2/Lt J.G. HURST to hospital.	
	9th		Route march. Preliminary note re move to I Corps area.	
	10th		Musketry party returned from TILQUES. D Orders from Bde received 10 p.m. Bn. left RICHED WORMHOUDT. - Marched to ESQUELBECQ, - entraining 9.18 a.m. Detrained BETHUNE 1 p.m. Marched to billets.	
ESQUELBECQ	11th		Bn. left BETHUNE 9 p.m. Marched to billets in ANNEQUIN. - settled by noon.	
BETHUNE	12th			
ANNEQUIN	13th		Bn. relieved 11th Bn ESSEX Regt in CAMBRIN LEFT-SECTOR, FRONT LINE, - Commencing 8 p.m. completed by 11 a.m.	
TRENCHES	14th–12th		Quiet. - nothing doing.	

CASUALTIES						
	Officers		Other Ranks			
	K.	W.	M.	K.	W.	M.
15th	—	1	—	1	3	1
17th	—	2	—	—	1	—

Army Form C. 2118.

WAR DIARY
or
INTELLIGENCE SUMMARY.
(Erase heading not required.)

Instructions regarding War Diaries and Intelligence Summaries are contained in F.S. Regs., Part II. and the Staff Manual respectively. Title pages will be prepared in manuscript.

Place	Date	Hour	Summary of Events and Information	Remarks and references to Appendices
				CASUALTIES
				Officers — Other ranks
				K. W. M. — K. W. M.
TRENCHES	19th	—	Bn. relieved by 15th D.L.I. commencing 1 pm; proceeded to Billets, ANNEQUIN	— — — — 3 —
ANNEQUIN	20th–23rd	—	Bn. in Reserve. Bn. Working parties, — cleaning & resting.	— 1 — — — —
TRENCHES	24th	—	Bn. relieved 15th D.L.I. in front line — A, B & B. Coys. Support — commenced 9 pm. "C" & "D" front line commenced 11 pm over the top owing to muddy state of trenches	
	25th to 28th	—	Quiet. — but much mud owing to front following thaw & trenches falling in. Tough time for carrying parties. 2/Lt P. D. ROOKE rejoined & 2/Lt P.T.O. MORRIS rejoined. B.O.R. reinforcements from 32nd I.B.D	4 1 1

1/3/17.

Certified true copy.

A.H. Burkett Capt & Adjutant
for Lt Col Comdg 10th (S) Bn. K.O.Y.L.I.

Army Form C. 2118.

WAR DIARY
or
INTELLIGENCE SUMMARY.
(Erase heading not required.)

15(S) Batt. K.O.Y.L.I.   Vol 19

Place	Date	Hour	Summary of Events and Information	Remarks and references to Appendices
	March 2	9 am	Battn. relieved by 15th D.L.I. in Cambrin Left Sector. Battn. proceeded to Support line relieving 9 K.O.Y.L.I. (1.30 pm)	
	3rd		In support.	
	5		Relieved by 1st Norfolk R. 12 mn. Battn. moved to BEURY arriving in billets 2.30 pm	
	6		Battn. moved to ROBECQ arriving in billets 2 pm. Light T.M. Course started (7 day)	
Robecq	7 + 8		Cleaning up & fitting of new clothing.	
	9		Battn. moved to BOUREÇQ arriving in billets 2.30 pm	
Bourecq	10			
	11	9 am	Battn. moved to PERNES arriving in billets 3 pm	
	12	9.30 am	" " HERICOURT arriving in billets 4 pm. Major Brown joined	
	13 14th 15th 16th 17th 18th	4.50 am	" " IVERGNY " " 3 pm	
			Training in new organization.	
IVERGNY	19	2 pm	Battn. moved to LE SOUICH arriving in billets vacated by 1st E. Yorks 3 pm	
	20		Coy Training	
	21		Coy Training. 2/Lt Mann rejoined from England.	
	22		Coy Training	
	23	10.25 am	Battn. moved to CONTEERA arriving 1.10 pm.	

Army Form C.2118.

WAR DIARY
or
INTELLIGENCE SUMMARY.
(Erase heading not required.)

Instructions regarding War Diaries and Intelligence Summaries are contained in F. S. Regs., Part II. and the Staff Manual respectively. Title pages will be prepared in manuscript.

Place	Date	Hour	Summary of Events and Information	Remarks and references to Appendices
GOMMERA	March 24, 25 & 26th		In training.	
	27		Batt moved to BERLES au-BOIS attached 62nd Inf. Bde.	
	28		Batt moved to ADINFER. Bivouac in wood. Batt working on road.	
HOINEER	29		Continued work on roads. ATS men	
	30		Continued work on roads. ATS men. 5pm batt moved to BOISLEUX au MONT	
Boisleux au Mont	31		Bivouaced in wood near railway. Constructed line of defence along sunken road S.29 & S.10. 2 from along railway from Boisleux to Hamelincourt.	

2353 Wt. W2544/1454 700,000 5/15 D. D. & L. A.D.S.S./Forms/C 2118.

SUBJECT.

64TH INF BDE
21ST DIV.

No.	Contents.	Date.

10TH BATT'N
K.O.Y.L.I.

WAR DIARY,
APRIL, 1917

WAR DIARY or INTELLIGENCE SUMMARY

Army Form C. 2118.

10th Bn KOYLI Vol 20

Place	Date	Hour	Summary of Events and Information	Remarks and references to Appendices
ROISLEUX AU MONT	April 1st & 2nd & 3rd		Battalion in bivouacs in the wood near the railway station. The battalion took over the left sector of the outpost line T.30.1.4 to T.9.2.55 from the 12th N.F. A Coy on the right with B Coy in support. C Coy on the right with D Coy in support.	April 3rd 3 OR wounded
"	April 4th 5th 6th		We remained in this line until the 8th. During this time much work was done. Two assembly trenches were dug in front & behind the road T.B.P. T.4.C. 9T.10.6. A large quantity of bombs, SAA & water were carried up and formed in to dumps in the assembly trenches and in the sunken road which we occupied. A great deal of patrolling was done to determine the amount of wire which was cut each day, & to report on the enemy held any posts in front of his wire & one patrol in particular is worthy of note. On the afternoon of the 7th Coy Sgt. Major Gill & Cpl Hammond of 7th Coy went out covered by a lewis gun. D.B. broad daylight while our artillery was shelling the German wire & line (HINDENBURG LINE) they walked 1500 yds up to the German wire. They walked along the German wire and made a careful inspection of it. They got back safely bringing with them very valuable information about the gaps which had been cut by our artillery. For this & other good service CSM Gill was awarded the DCM & Cpl Hammond the Military Medal. 2nd Lieut Hobbs (killed on the night of the 10th) was in charge of the Lewis Gun. 2nd Lieut Cundall of A Coy & 2nd Lieut Fox of C Coy. On the night of the 8th April the 9th K.O.Y.L.I. the 15th D.L.I. and 1st E Yorks took up their positions in the jumping off trenches which had been dug. The 9th went on the left the 15th in the centre & the 1st E Yorks on the right. The 10th K.O.Y.L.I. remained in their old positions in the Sunken Road T.30.1.4. to T.9.2.55. Batt. Hd.Qrs. moved from S.18.b.77. to T.14.d.4.7. 46 men of C Coy were attached as a carrying party to 64th M.G. Coy. 4th Bde attacked the Hindenburg line in the afternoon. 2nd Lieut Cundall & 30 men of A Coy were attached to the 1st E Yorks as a carrying party 2nd Lieut Sharp & 30 men of D Coy were attached to 15th D.L.I. & 2nd Lieut Wray & 30 men of B Coy to 9th K.O.Y.L.I. Batt. were in Bde reserve.	April 6th 1 OR wounded Capt W M Penny R.A.M.C. wounded 5 OR wounded April 7th 1 OR wounded April 8th 2 OR wounded
	April 9th			

Army Form C. 2118.

Answered N 34 A54
B.V.26
69

WAR DIARY
or
INTELLIGENCE SUMMARY
(Erase heading not required.)

Instructions regarding War Diaries and Intelligence Summaries are contained in F. S. Regs., Part II. and the Staff Manual respectively. Title Pages will be prepared in manuscript.

Place	Date	Hour	Summary of Events and Information	Remarks and references to Appendices
	April 9th	7.30 pm	At about 7.30 pm A & C Coys under Capt Marat were sent up to reinforce the 1st E.Yorks & 15 D.L.I. who had succeeded in penetrating the Hindenburg Line and were holding about 1000 yds from T.5.a.3.4. & N.3.d.6.5. A difficult operation which was carried out successfully in the dark. B & D Coys under Capt Hitchcock were sent up to occupy the Sunken road just outside the German wire.	Casualties April 9th 2nd Lieut Hobbs killed 2nd Lieut Wimman killed 2nd Lieuts Murrie P.S.O. Yardley E.B. Sharp H.E. wounded O.R. killed 10, missing 14, wounded 41. 17
		11.30 pm	About 11.30 pm Lt. Col. P.O'B. Thirkeld was ordered to establish his HdQrs in the piece of Hindenburg line behind the Sunken road occupied by B & D Coys & to hold the line until the situation was instructed as affected on the situation. After making a tour of the line & he could satisfy himself that his battalion he reported that a disorganising night. The situation with the officers of each battalion he reported that a disorganising night.	
			In the meantime the 126th & Coy RE under the personal supervision of Major Shakespeare RE together with the 14 MT progressively tried to establish in rear of the Sunken road occupied by B & D coys. The Bde instructed Cow Cpl to extend their wire thence from the Sunken road HdQr in the westernmost.	
	10th	3.30 am	139 D Coys took up their communication position together with Bn HdQr in the westernmost position. Together with 50 men of the 126th & Co. RE we dug a communication trench from the new trench to the German front line. C. Coy of the 10th R.O.Y.L.I. relieved the bombing posts of the 15th D.L.I. on the left & held the line from the communication trench to the left of the captured line.	
		8 am	C. Coy repulsed a very determined hostile bombing attack throwing over 300 bombs. Pte Waller of C. Coy distinguished himself on this occasion. Although wounded he stuck to his post and continued bombing until he died. He has been recommended for a Victoria Cross. During the day rations, water & a very large supply of bombs were brought up by parties from each coy. The party under 2/Lt W my did exceptionally well in this respect. Hot tea and rum was issued of the men. The dispositions of the battalions are shown in the sketch below.	

```
                                        M Coy 10 R.O.Y.LI.      1st E Yorks
                                        xxxxxxxxxxxxxxxxxx
Block   C.Coy 10 R.O.Y.LI.  15th DLI  xxxxxxxxxxxxx
xxxxxxxxxxxx
                    ← New Comm inundation trench
            B & D Coys
            B Coy 1st ←--→ new trench
                         Sunken road
                         B Coy
```

2449   Wt. W14957/M90   750,000   1/16   J.B.C. & A.   Forms/C.2118/12.

WAR DIARY or INTELLIGENCE SUMMARY

Army Form C. 2118.

Place	Date	Hour	Summary of Events and Information	Remarks and references to Appendices
	April 10th		About 4 p.m. the enemy attacked all the posts in the left sub section early morning in addition to infantry attack from rifle grenades, air trench mortars which fired shells about the size of Stokes. The right section had a by some means to return. The Lieuts 2 Lieuts Holt & Warner were killed.	
			When organising resistance & serving bombs. C by feel en route all the others had returned into 3 battalion informed we - the no trench & prepared to counterattack.	
			As soon as the 10th E York began to come back the artillery opened up. The above mentioned in our front line to the artillery to left so that a counter attack could be made & through the R.E. machine no 5 machine guns were on the 62 nd Bde. & the same time a message came through from the R.E. machine no 5 machine guns were on the Bde.	
			was on their way up to relieve us.	
Bosuy Becquerelle	11th 12th 13th	Early morning	eg. We were relieved by the 62 d Bde. a unit from to BOIRY BECOUERELLE. Battn remained in BOIRY BECQUERELLE. During this time a great deal of saluting was done. We succeeded in burying a large portion of the bodies of the men who had been killed	
FICHEUX	14th	10 p.m.	Battalion marched to FICHEUX & bivouaced & dugouts.	
	15th 16th 17th 18th		Battalion remained in FICHEUX.	
Bosuy au Mont	19th 20th 21st	1 p.m.	Battalion moved to BOISLEUX au MONT & bivouaced near the railway on embankment. John 3 Coys working on the roads where the other Coy. was at BLAIRVILLE pulling No 28118 CSM J Gill I.W.L 13286 Cpl A HAMMOND, S/4742 L/Cpl R RUMFITT. 30144 Pte H WALKER (killed) answered Roll Commander Court.	
	22		16327 Q Q J DARBY 5 p.m.	
	23		Received sudden orders to move to MERCATEL. Arrived 5 a.m. Bivouaced Received sudden orders to move to BOIRY BECQUERELLE. Arrived 5 a.m. Bivouaced	
	24		Battalion relieved 20th Bn Royal Fusiliers who were holding an out post line from Hindenburg support line ½ (T.6.a.4.M) to Number one trench road (O.31.C.18). The relief was carried out just before dark to the way up the trenches was rather heavily shelled and there were a number of casualties	April 25th 2 OR killed
	25			2 OR killed 6 OR wounded

Army Form C.2118.

WAR DIARY
or
INTELLIGENCE SUMMARY
(Erase heading not required.)

Instructions regarding War Diaries and Intelligence Summaries are contained in F. S. Regs., Part II. and the Staff Manual respectively. Title Pages will be prepared in manuscript.

Place	Date	Hour	Summary of Events and Information	Remarks and references to Appendices
Front line	April 26		C & D Coys under Capt Dexter held the front line and A,B & B Coys under Capt Sheffield remained in outpost. The front line consisted of some 12 strong posts ground together in some cases by a shallow trench. This line was on the forward slope of the hill overlooking FONTAINE les CROISILLES and was under almost observation from the enemy. Both the front & support Coys were shelled fairly heavily during the day. During the night 26/27 a great deal of work was done in entrenching the front lines & digging up the men of the strong post. A large number of the 33rd Division were found & no less a large quantity of salvage work	
	27		Still a fair amount of shelling. Men worked hard burying the dead & salvaging equipment & ammunition. Large numbers of German dead were also buried. Returns were brought in number so far as Bn HQrs. Work on front line continued during the night & a line of wire was started in front. Enemy shelled our posting heavily. Salvage work & burial of dead continued.	April 28 2nd Lieut J.A. HINCHCLIFFE attached 6th TMB Bty wounded 5 OR Killed 22 OR wounded
	28		During the night work continued on the front line. It was impossible for large parties about near the front line during the day with MT heavy shelled. Rations brought up on mules to Ruth the C.O.T. & mules died by supply Coy to the line. A & B Coys relieved C & D in front line after dark. Rather quieter than on previous days.	April 29 3 OR wounded
	29			
	30		No 16327 Pte J DARBY and No 34992 L/Cpl R RUMFITT awarded the Military Medal. Totally quiet.	

A.H. Burkett Capt.
a/adjutant
for Lt. Col. Cmg 10th N.O.Y.L.I.

2449 Wt. W14957/M90 750,000 1/16 J.B.C. & A. Forms/C.2118/12.

Army Form C. 2118.

WAR DIARY
or
INTELLIGENCE SUMMARY
(Erase heading not required.)

10th Bn K.O.Y.L.I.   Vol 21

21.M.
3 sheets

Place	Date	Hour	Summary of Events and Information	Remarks and references to Appendices
The Line	May 1st 1917		A & B Coys in Boom Trench overlooking MONTAINE LES CROISILLES. C & D Coys in Support. Battalion relieved by 110 Bde & moved into reserve in HINDENBURG Support Line. Men very tired and badly in need of a bath.	6
	2nd		Men washed & refitted in afternoon. Battalion kept in reserve near BULLE COURT.	4
			Moved up in the evening in support of 15th DLI. A Coy under Capt HNG HAYCOCK in the HINDENBURG Front Line. B, C & D Coys in the HINDENBURG Support Line.	1
	3rd	3.15 am	After short bombardment attack opened. 15th DLI supported by 10th KOYLI to bomb down HINDENBURG Line. 110th Bde to attack over the open N of HINDENBURG Support Line. 62nd Division to make a further attack on HINDENBURG Line to west of BULLECOURT, 1st Australian Div supporting. 110th Bde put out of action at once. The tank supporting 62nd Inf Bde. and 63 Bgde & tanks had to move down parallel to the HINDENBURG Support line in order to keep direction. Tank reached our fence just in front of action by enemy trench mortar. The Trench beyond the enemy block was found to be full of wire and the first bombing squad of the DLI who went on were snipered who had taken up their positions near the block did a great deal of damage as the men climbed over the top. We failed to make any headway in the HINDENBURG Support Line. On the front line, a Coy of the DLI & some bombers of May under 2/Lt Aundale pushed forward about 200 yds but were driven back to their original position & also failed to make any headway, Position remained the same throughout the day. 110th Bde got no further with Trench west of SENSÉE River but were driven out later in the day. 2/Lt Aundale was killed whilst leading his bombers. Capt HNG HAYCOCK was killed & a shell burst after ZERO hour. 15th DLI were relieved by 1/5th E. Yorks in the evening.	9, 47, 2

Army Form C.2118.

WAR DIARY
or
INTELLIGENCE SUMMARY
(Erase heading not required.)

Instructions regarding War Diaries and Intelligence Summaries are contained in F. S. Regs., Part II. and the Staff Manual respectively. Title Pages will be prepared in manuscript.

Place	Date	Hour	Summary of Events and Information	Remarks and references to Appendices
In the Line	Aug 4		Relieved by the 9th Royal Sussex with reserve Coy. Then rest of men got their nights rest, wash & shave.	
	5		In reserve. Major Brown came up & took over from Col Postlethwaite who needed a rest.	
	6		In reserve.	
	7		Relieved the 15th Div. who were holding the flank in the Hindenburg Line.	
	8		Consolidated our position. Built fire steps facing North. Sniper did good work down gun post established in captured trench.	
	9			
	10			
	11		Relieved at 6 p.m. by 4th Kings Liverpool Regiment. Marched to Boisleux St Marc Boundary. Bivouac hut & bivouaced for the night.	
	12		All the men had a bath & a clean change.	
	13	3.30 p.m	"Battalion" marched to rest billets at Berles Court. Church Parade.	
	14		Commenced Coy. Training. 6 a.m – 8.30 am 9am 12.30 pm afternoon free. Coy an all firing on the range. Training awarded Rugby of Musketry.	
	15 16 16½			
	17		Battalion Sports in the afternoon.	
	18		Coy training. Practiced training attack down over ground front line.	
	19			
	20		Rifle Sports in the afternoon. Coy won the Tug of War.	
	21 22 23		Continued Coy training & practiced attack down trenches.	
	24			
	25		Practice frontal attack on trenches with whole Battalion.	
	26		Brigadier watched a practice frontal attack	

Army Form C. 2118.

WAR DIARY
or
INTELLIGENCE SUMMARY

(Erase heading not required.)

Instructions regarding War Diaries and Intelligence Summaries are contained in F. S. Regs., Part II. and the Staff Manual respectively. Title Pages will be prepared in manuscript.

Place	Date	Hour	Summary of Events and Information	Remarks and references to Appendices
BELLACOURT	May 27		Training mostly much interrupted. Church Parade.	
	28		Divisional Commander watched practice frontal attack. Battalion inspected by Corps Commander in the afternoon. Sgt Ham, Sgt Musgrove & Sgt Nash given the Military Medal. Hope Sandhurst in hospital so could not receive his Military Medal from the Corps Commander.	
	29.		Training continued. Warning order for move received.	
	30		Day spent in cleaning up.	
	31	2.30p	Battalion moved to BOYELLES.	

H. Birkett Capt
Adjutant
10 H KOYLI

2449 Wt. W14957/M90 750,000 1/16 J.B.C. & A. Forms/C.2118/12.

WAR DIARY or INTELLIGENCE SUMMARY

Army Form C. 2118.

10TH (S) BATTALION. K.O.Y.L.I.
No. X. 11.
Date 2.7.17.

Place	Date	Hour	Summary of Events and Information	Remarks and references to Appendices
BOYELLES.	1917 JUNE. 1.		Battalion occupying bivouacs at BOYELLES. 'C' Company detached under command of 9th Bn K.O.Y.L.I in front line. Remaining companies carrying out training for open warfare. Training of bombers, Lewis gunners and other specialists continued.	
"	2.		Training continued – A, B and C Companies doing practice attacks, storming of trenches etc.	
"	3.		Training. Inspections of arms, equipments etc prior to moving into trenches. 11 other ranks, reinforcements, joined.	
"	4.		Captain the Revd. F S MARSH joined as Chaplain.	
"	"		Battalion moved into area T.9.d. and T.10.c. occupying dug outs, pioneer jumpits and bivouacs, as Battalion in Brigade Reserve.	
"	5.	6 a.m 6.30 a.m	Battalion Headquarters shelled by heavy H.E. shells. Captain and Adjutant H. BURKETT severely wounded near sunken road about T.9.d.8.8. whilst supervising arrangements for bivouacs for Headquarters Staff. The Rev. Captain BURKETT died of wounds on arrival at Field Ambulance. Captain BURKETT was carried from the Field Ambulance to HENIN	1 3

Army Form C.118.

WAR DIARY or INTELLIGENCE SUMMARY.

(Erase heading not required.)

Instructions regarding War Diaries and Intelligence Summaries are contained in F. S. Regs., Part II. and the Staff Manual respectively. Title pages will be prepared in manuscript.

Place	Date	Hour	Summary of Events and Information	Remarks and references to Appendices
	1917 JUNE		(continued)	
	5.		Military Cemetery, by Headquarters Staff Sergeants and buried; No. 7832 Private A.C. WRENN, who was killed during this bombardment was buried at the same time, the Brigadier-General commanding the 144th Inf. Brigade and representatives from each Battalion in the Brigade being present at these funerals. Private WRENN, a very fine soldier, and a nature of MONS, landed in France with the original British Expeditionary Force and had taken part in most of the principal engagements of the War.	
	5.	7.30 a.m.	During the bombardment of Battalion Headquarters No.14426. Cpl. F. BROWN a stretcher bearer remained alone in the open with a dangerously wounded man and coolly applied the necessary first aid until the patient could be moved. Cpl. BROWN has since been awarded the Military Medal for this act.	
	6–7.		Time occupied by general fitting up and cleaning etc. preparatory to moving into Front Line Trenches.	
	7.		Reconnaissance of Front Line by Officers.	1

Army Form C. 118.

WAR DIARY
or
INTELLIGENCE SUMMARY.
(Erase heading not required.)

Instructions regarding War Diaries and Intelligence Summaries are contained in F.S. Regs., Part II. and the Staff Manual respectively. Title pages will be prepared in manuscript.

Place	Date	Hour	Summary of Events and Information	Remarks and references to Appendices
	1917		(continued)	Officers / Other Ranks
				K W M K W M
	JUNE 8th		Battalion moved into front line relieving 15th. Batt. Durham Light Infantry. In carrying out this relief the Battalion suffered casualties - 2 O.R. killed and 6 O.R. wounded, by the intense activity of hostile artillery. Owing to a raid being carried out on the night it is thought that these casualties might have been avoided had the Battalion been warned of this intended raid.	2 6
Front line	9th	10-11	Enemy just normally active. Our troops constantly patrolling the front, but very little to report. Large fighting patrols out each night, also parties digging, widening and generally improving trenches.	
			2/Lieuts. HUTSON and SLATER joined. 13 Other ranks, reinforcements joined.	
	10		Whilst Battalion was in reserve small classes of Lewis Gunners & Bombers were being trained at transport lines, as reserves.	
" "	9-15			
	13.		Battalion relieved in front line by 1st. Bn. East York. Regt. at midnight, and marched to BOYELLES to bivouacs. Relief successfully accomplished without casualties, by 2 am.	

3

WAR DIARY or INTELLIGENCE SUMMARY.

Army Form C. 2118.

Place	Date	Hour	Summary of Events and Information	Remarks and references to Appendices
	1917 JUNE			
BOYELLES	13		Resting and cleaning up after tour in trenches.	
"	14 & 15		Training continued.	
"	16.		17 Battalion buglers under Lieut. G.H. WRAY blew the "charge" from the fire-step for the attack on TUNNEL TRENCH, from the HINDENBURG LINE by the 110th Infantry Brigade, afterwards taking cover from the hostile artillery barrage. The buglers successfully sounded the "Charge" without casualties.	
			Battalion moved to support trenches relieving 15th Bn. Durham. L.I. at 10. p.m. Relief accomplished without casualties.	
	17.		Battalion in support. traditions remark.	
	18.		" " "	
	18 - 19.		" " "	
	19.		Specialists instructional classes continued at transport lines whilst Batt. in support. Battalion relieved at midnight by 4th Bn. Kings Liverpool Regt. and marched to bivouacs at BOYELLES.	
BOYELLES	20.		Morning – resting, afternoon taken up by cleaning and packing up ready for move. Battalion marched off at 8 pm. by platoons at	

Army Form C. 2118.

WAR DIARY
or
INTELLIGENCE SUMMARY.
(Erase heading not required.)

Place	Date	Hour	Summary of Events and Information	Remarks and references to Appendices
	1917 June		(Continued)	
POMMIER	21-22-23		200 yards intervals to POMMIER. In billets by 12 midnight. 3 days devoted to resting, cleaning up and replacing deficiencies in kits etc. Recreational training such as football, cricket, rounders etc commenced.	
"	23.		2nd Lieutenants BLACKBURN, MAGIN and BARNES and six other ranks joined as reinforcements.	
"	24-25		Morning hours occupied by physical drill, arms drill, wiring drill, musketry training, firing on ranges etc. Afternoons devoted to recreational training, games & concerts.	
"	26-27-28		Training continued, as for 24th & 25th inst.	
"	28th		2nd Lieuts HARRISON and ROWLAND joined. Four other ranks joined as reinforcements.	
"	29th		Battalion left POMMIER at 3.15 a.m. for MOYENNEVILLE, arriving 6.45 a.m. and taking over Camp "A" from 1st Bn. Scottish Rifles.	
MOYENNEVILLE	30		Battalion resting during day. Marched off at 8 p.m. to support trenches relieving 2nd Bn. Worcester Regt. Information received that No.31440. Private H. WALKER had been	

WAR DIARY
or
INTELLIGENCE SUMMARY.
(Erase heading not required.)

Army Form C. 118.

Place	Date	Hour	Summary of Events and Information	Remarks and references to Appendices
			(Continued) awarded the VICTORIA CROSS for most conspicuous bravery when with a bombing section forming a block in the enemy line 10/4/17. A very violent counter attack was made by the enemy on this post and although five of the garrison were killed Private WALKER continued for more than an hour to throw bombs and finally repulsed the attack. In the morning he swung his swing again counter-attacked the post and all the garrison became casualties except PR. WALKER who although wounded later continued to throw bombs for another half an hour until he was killed. Throughout these attacks he showed the utmost valour and it was due to his determination that the attacks on this important post were repulsed. 2.9.17.	

G.A. Brews Major
for O.C. 10th Bn. K.O.Y.L.I.

Army Form C.2118.

WAR DIARY or INTELLIGENCE SUMMARY

10th Bn K.O.Y.L.I.

Nov 23

(Erase heading not required.)

Instructions regarding War Diaries and Intelligence Summaries are contained in F.S. Regs., Part II. and the Staff Manual respectively. Title Pages will be prepared in manuscript.

23.M.
5 sheets

Place	Date	Hour	Summary of Events and Information	Remarks and references to Appendices
SUPPORT LINE RIGHT SECTOR OF DIV FRONT	JULY 1	4.	"A", "B" and "D" Coys held trenches behind CROISILLES, The trenches running from T.23.c.8.10. to T.23.c.67. (Ref Sh18.S.W 1/20,000) and "C" Company in Sunken Road running from T.23.a.5.6 to T.23.c.6.9. Bn. H.Q in Road at T.23.c.6.9. Conditions Normal. Intermittent Shelling of Battalion in the vicinity on our right. Trenches were improved, also Communication New dugouts made in road at Bn. Hd. Qrs.	Officers K.W.M. O.Ranks K.W.M.
	2nd		"C" Company in Sunken Road carried out L.G. practice each morning. 3 Other Ranks joined as reinforcements.	
	1 - 4		Specialists (sic) Platoons Classes were organized with useless party at Inceptes Line.	
Front Line	4.		Left Support Line at 4 p.m. to relieve the 15th Durham Light Infantry in the left Sub-sector of the Right Sector of Divisional Front extending from U.7.b.15.72. on the left to V.7.a.2.0. on the right. Relief successfully carried out without casualties by 7 p.m.	
	5		Working parties wiring during night of 4th & 5th. Enemy gave very little opportunity for sniping but those of the enemy were observed to have been hit by our men.	
	6		Conditions Normal, then busy improving trenches during the day, also carrying were Stay wiring parties out during the night. Conditions Normal. Kept a keen look out for any opportunities for sniping but enemy very careful not to expose himself. Aeroplane flew low over our lines but quickly disappeared on our aeroplane appearing. 2 O.R. very slightly wounded from Rifle Grenade fire. Our artillery very active, constantly dispersing parties of the enemy in the bad area. Our own T.M. 13's also fired very successfully.	

WAR DIARY or INTELLIGENCE SUMMARY

Army Form C.2118.

Place	Date	Hour	Summary of Events and Information	Remarks and references to Appendices
	6th		(Continued) Wiring parties out during the night of the 6th-7th. Suffered no casualties. Conditions normal. Hostile aeroplanes flew low over our lines but were quickly driven off by our anti-aircraft gun & machine gun fire. Their aeroplanes during the day reporting trenches & strong enemy wiring parties out during the night. These reconnaissance patrols were sent out at night to report on enemy positions & wire etc. From their reports it was evident that the enemy were no on the whole only fair, being very spotty in places. From our own observations & patrol reports it is evident that the enemy is holding his front line with machine guns. These caliberes fire but have been seen at night mounted on their parapet.	Other Ranks
	7th		The enemy patrols seen.	1
	7th & 8th		2 Other Ranks very slightly wounded by Rifle Grenade fire, 1 remaining at duty. Wiring parties out during the night of 7th-8th.	2
	8th		Conditions normal. 3 other ranks two slightly wounded by Rifle Grenade fire, 1 remaining at duty. Hostile Mining suspected towards MEIZUS at the East End of JUMPS LINE. Mining registers heard there and 5.9's. Enemy very active. Our own artillery very active. Several whizzbangs & aerial darts fired by enemy. At 2 p.m. the Battalion was relieved in the front line by the 6th Leicester Regiment. Relief successfully carried out without casualties & completed by 5.30 p.m. Battalion proceeded on relief to Camp "C" MOVENVILLE into Brigade Reserve.	
MOVENVILLE	4th-5th	9th	During the period the Battalion was in the front line the specialists instructional classes were continued. Day devoted to resting, cleaning up, bathing etc. Recreational training such as football & cricket commenced.	
		10th	2nd/Lieuts PHKKE, BEHR, and WALTER joined as reinforcements. TRAINING. Morning occupied by bayonet fighting, physical drill & arms drill	

2449 Wt. W14957/M90 750,000 1/16 J.B.C. & A. Forms/C.2118/12.

WAR DIARY or INTELLIGENCE SUMMARY

(Erase heading not required.)

Army Form C. 2118.

Place	Date	Hour	Summary of Events and Information	Remarks and references to Appendices
	10th		and evening practice. Afternoon devoted to Recreational Training. Cricket v/s Captain L.B.SPICER joined from 2/4th K.O.Y.L.I. and appointed Adjutant.	
	11th		1 O.R. joined as reinforcement.	
			Training continued. Company drill + artillery formation practised. Kit Inspection. Afternoon & evening devoted to Recreational Training. Cpl/Lce. G.LOCKWOOD found	
	12th		Training continued. Special Attention paid to saluting in view of a Bde swimming competition due to come off at the end of the week. In the afternoon at Officers cricket match was played against the 9th K.O.Y.L.I. in which we were defeated by 3 runs.	
	13th		Training Continued.	
	14th		Training continued. In the evening Bde Swimming Competition was held. This was won by 9th K.O.Y.L.I. + this Battalion was second. A Regimental Cricket match was played against the 1st East Yorks, which we won quite easily.	
	15th		Church Parade in the morning. No parades otherwise. Draft E.SLATER and transferred to 9th Bn K.O.Y.L.I. which he had originally joined.	
	16th		Bn. moved into Bde Reserve at BOYELLES. Two Coys "A" (under Capt MSIM) and "D" (under Capt DEXTER) held the front line, relief complete 10 (Afterns), there were last casualties. Our line it had been heavily shelled, but reinforcing of the new. Our live Coys worked on the evening manning parties up to the front. At night live Coys sent working parties to work at UNKNOWN TRENCH + FIRST AVENUE. The two Coys at BOYELLES continued training.	
	20th		Battalion relieved at 15th D.I.I. in the front line, in the left sector of the Bde line. Our line ran from U.1.a central to O.31.d central. It was by no means a straight line, but was full of re-entrants.	

Sgd/ T. NORMANTON Maj. The Battalion.

2449 Wt. W14957/M90 750,000 1/16 J.B.C. & A. Forms/C.2118/12.

WAR DIARY
or
INTELLIGENCE SUMMARY

(Erase heading not required.)

Army Form C.2118.

Instructions regarding War Diaries and Intelligence Summaries are contained in F.S. Regs., Part II. and the Staff Manual respectively. Title Pages will be prepared in manuscript.

Place	Date	Hour	Summary of Events and Information	Remarks and references to Appendices
	21st		Work consisted of every which was badly need & in improvement of existing trenches. This was carried on.	
	22nd		Nothing of particular importance occurred. Their movement seems to come from Thier trenches N.E. FONTAINE, + great opportunity for sniping was given, though the range was rather long. Rifles over 900 yards. 1 O.R. killed. Except the rather ranged the ... Boy H.Q. "D" Coy (near Copse DEXTER) was ... not very troublesome. The particular place mentioned (O.91.C.76) was ... ... had largely owing to the fact that there was a rabbit close by, which ... ... essential to the enemy person. We alone however much troubled by arial darts, which (the	
	23rd		artillery fired	1
	24th		enemy fired at our centre + left Coy line. At 10.30am in the morning the enemy opened a heavy fire with arial darts on our advanced posts at V1 and 71 (approx) This fort was no na isolated post which could only be reached by "D" Coy HQ by two ... It was fused by "D" Boy who used the command of 2nd/Lt BARNES. At 1am the enemy opened a heavy fire, and at 1.15am 2nd/Lt BARNES was killed. Sgt SYKES at once took charge of the situation to Boy H.Q. + got the men to have at forget leaving the enemy night attempt a raid. The fire did not slacken till 3.30 and at about 4.15am we got the artillery on to the troublesome area + in so an calling the fire ceased. Great credit is due to Sgt SYKES for the cool way in which he handled the situation. The fire also fell on the trenches held by "B" Coy under 2nd/Lt WRAY. 2nd/Lt BARNES killed, no O.R. killed, 3 O.R. wounded.	1. 2. 3.
	25th		Lt.Col. F.J.M. POSTLETHWAITE admitted to Hospital. The Bn. was relieved by the 1st LINCOLNS + moved into Divisional Reserve at MOYENNEVILLE	
	27th	5pm	The day was spent cleaning up. In the evening a riding school was started for Officers + horses very popular. Tactical exercises for Battalion Officers at Risl	

2449 Wt. W14957/M90 750,000 1/16 J.B.C. & A. Forms/C.2118/12.

Army Form C. 2118.

WAR DIARY
or
INTELLIGENCE SUMMARY
(Erase heading not required.)

Place	Date	Hour	Summary of Events and Information	Remarks and references to Appendices
	27th 28th		(Brig General MERIDAM was present). Training continued. Tactical Exercise for Infantry Officers held at artist S.O.B.	
	29th 30th 31st		(MAJOR GENERAL CAMPBELL was present). Colonel Paradis reached the Battalion. Sgt Sykes awarded the Military Medal for his gallant behaviour on the 26th inst. Brigadier General MERIDAM conducted a tactical exercise with Officers of the Battalion. In conjunction with the 9th R.O.H.L. Regimental Sports were held. These should of course have been held at MINDEN DAY (Aug 1st), but owing to our having to move into the line on that day this was impossible.	

J.D. Shind
Capt & Adjt
8th R.O.Y.L.

WAR DIARY 10th KOYLI
or
INTELLIGENCE SUMMARY.
(Erase heading not required.)

Army Form C.2118.

10TH (S) BATTALION.,
K.O.Y.L.I.
No. X.15
Date 2.9.17

Place	Date	Hour	Summary of Events and Information	Remarks and references to Appendices
SUPPORT LINE RIGHT SECTOR.	1917 AUGUST 1st		Battalion left MOYENNEVILLE Camp to relieve the 7th Bn. LEICESTER REGT in support in the right sector. "A" Coy under Capt. MEIN relieving "A" Coy 7th LEICESTERS in the Quarry T.18.d.97, "B" Coy under Capt. HOLDSTOCK relieving "B" Coy. "C" Coy under Lieut. FOX relieving "C" Coy, & "D" Coy under Capt. DEXTER relieving "D" Coy, the last three being in the area T.23. central. Relief successfully carried out without casualties by 11 p.m. "B" Coy in Cardon Trench T.23.a. central, "C" & "D" Coy in trenches behind T.23.a.7.4. - T.23.a.6.1., "B" Hd Qrs in Sunken Road T.23.C.28 - T.23.d.13/5.	Officers K.W.M. Other Ranks K.W.M.
	2nd		About 10 p.m. 1 O.R. hit by shell fire & dies of wounds the following morning. 1 O.R. wounded. Several working parties found by Battalion. Remainder employed improving trenches & c. Capt. F.H.P. DEXTER admitted to Hospital.	1. 1.
	3rd		At 4 a.m. enemy attempted to raid the 15th D.L.I. by the METRU in LUMPLINE. Attack repulsed and Lewis gun & Rifle fire. Working parties sent out as before.	
	4th		2nd/Lt. J.W. DORE joined and 2 O.R. Working of importance to record. Working parties as event.	
	5th		2 O.R. killed and 2 O.R. wounded by Shell fire in the vicinity of the QUARRY.	
	6th		Nothing of importance to record. Working parties Cont and as before.	

WAR DIARY or INTELLIGENCE SUMMARY

Army Form C. 118.

Place	Date	Hour	Summary of Events and Information	Remarks and references to Appendices
FRONT LINE CENTRE SECTOR	AUGUST 1st	1 am	The Battalion left SUPPORT LINE to relieve the 1st SOUTH STAFFORDSHIRE REGT in the front line in the centre sector of the New Brigade, and — the right of the Battn line being at U.20.a.10.5 exclusive and the lft of the Battn line being at U.14.a.0.1. inclusive. Bn. Hd Qrs at T.24.d.7.4. Disposition of Coys as follows:- "A" Coy in STRAHGEWAYS RESERVE. "B" Coy in the left sector front line. "C" Coy in the right sector front line. "D" Coy in Reserve at Bn. Hd Qrs. Relief successfully carried out without casualties by 10.45 a.m. 1 O.R. sent to England as candidate for commission.	
	8th	Between 1.30 am and 2 am the support line of the Battn on our right was shelled at irregular intervals. At 1.15 a.m. an enemy patrol of 20-25 men moving in file towards our line. They were spotted by the covering party to our wirers. Fire was opened on them & nothing further was seen or heard. Drive day. 1 O.R sent to ENGLAND as candidate for a commission.	
	9th	At 3.30 a.m. men between front line & Strangeways shelled for a while found at the back of N range for hours. Enemy active at intervals throughout the day with aerial darts on front line trenches. C.S.M. YOUNGSTON & SGT. CHERRY wounded. The Battalion extended its left to the —nen Red. Boundary at junction of NELLY LANE	2

WAR DIARY or INTELLIGENCE SUMMARY

Army Form C. 118.

		Summary of Events and Information	Remarks and references to Appendices
Place	Date / Hour		

10- and BURG TRENCH. "A" & "C" Coys being relieved by two Companies of the 9th K.O.Y.L.I. and "B" Coy relieving right front Coy, left sub-Sector, 1st EAST YORKSHIRE REGT. "D" Coy relieving right front Coy, left sub-Sector, 1st EAST YORKS. "D" Coy moving into support in LINCOLN TRENCH. Relief successfully carried out without casualties to our Batt. By 1 p.m. during the relief one of the 9th K.O.Y.L.I. KNUCKLE AVENUE was heavily shelled, destroying the trench & burying the telephone wires in many places. Two of our signallers No. 13501 Pt. R.P. SIDDLE and No. 13641 Pt. C. COWEN who were Lineman mended the wires in spite of the Bombardment, and great coolness disregard of danger. They refused to be relieved until the line "For the credit of the Batt." could be handed over in good working order and after that voluntarily remained for about 3 hours longer assisting the Linesmen of the 9th K.O.Y.L.I. to maintain communication in that area. The example was a very fine one. These men have since been awarded the MILITARY MEDAL for this action.

11- From 10 a.m. to 12 noon FACTORY AVENUE was intermittently shelled in salvoes of 3. Several stand fired on our front line at intervals throughout the day, the most falling round our right Coy. H.Q. Our TRENCH MORTARS were active on Enemy front line - Good shooting

WAR DIARY
or
INTELLIGENCE SUMMARY.
(Erase heading not required.)

Army Form C. 118.

Place	Date	Hour	Summary of Events and Information	Remarks and references to Appendices
	AUGUST 12th		At 11.45 a.m. aerial darts were fired in rapid succession round our left Coy H.Q. At 2 p.m. again at 9.10 p.m. KELLY AVENUE and LINCOLN TRENCH were shelled for a short period at the rate of 4 rounds per minute. Our Artillery & Trench Mortars active on enemy trenches.	
	13th		From 6.45 a.m. to Noon Battalion Headquarters were heavily shelled at the rate of about 2 rounds every 3 minutes. 1 O.R. At 7.25 p.m. aerial darts were fired in rapid succession round our left Coy H.Q. Our trench mortars and aerial darts were active on enemy front line throughout the 24 hours.	
	14th		Our 18 pounders were very active on enemy wire & front line, also our Heavy Trench Mortars Knocked at the junction of FAS HALEY and TUNNEL TRENCH junction which have been very badly damaged. Also our aerial darts very active during the day. Other wise nothing of importance to record. 2 O.R. wounded.	2
	15th		From 1.55 to 2.20 a.m. the enemy shelled BERNHAM'S LOOP and our right Coy Hd Qrs. and 5.96, 4.26 a.m TRENCH MORTARS the whole being covered by about 30 t 60 M.C.M shells. Seno firing from UPTON WOOD. There were no casualties this damage was done. Again from 4 am to 4.15 am the area from the Loop to KNUCKLE AVENUE	

WAR DIARY or INTELLIGENCE SUMMARY.

(Erase heading not required.)

Army Form C. 2118.

Instructions regarding War Diaries and Intelligence Summaries are contained in F. S. Regs., Part II. and the Staff Manual respectively. Title pages will be prepared in manuscript.

Place	Date	Hour	Summary of Events and Information	Remarks and references to Appendices
	15th		was killed with H.Q. H.E. and Shrapnel. No casualties. No damage was done. Our T.M's active on enemy trenches twice. 2nd Lieut. H.F. WYNNE proceeded to R.F.C. as observer on probation.	
	16th		2nd Lieut. G.H. SHEPHERDSON joined. 6 O.R. joined. At 8.55 a.m. a hostile airing party two (see map the MERU at V.M.A.1.7, and a covering party was also out with a white flag. Our STOKES MORTAR landed a number of shots well into the middle of the party & the first shot sent them away the white flag. The party scattered & the firing was then directed on to the main party in rear mounting in slight retaliation from light artillery. Our artillery particularly 18 pounders very active on enemy trenches twice. Enemy artillery fairly quiet. The Battalion was relieved in the front line by the 1st Batt. EAST YORKS. Relief Regt. Battalion moved into PATRICIA CAMP, ERVILLERS.	
PATRICIA CAMP.	17th 18th		Successfully carried out entrain casualties and complete by 11 p.m. Bn. resting & clearing up. Men bathing. Racing programme commenced. Recreation in the evening	

Army Form C.118.

WAR DIARY
or
INTELLIGENCE SUMMARY.
(Erase heading not required.)

Instructions regarding War Diaries and Intelligence Summaries are contained in F. S. Regs., Part II. and the Staff Manual respectively. Title pages will be prepared in manuscript.

Place	Date	Hour	Summary of Events and Information	Remarks and references to Appendices
	18th		1 O.R. sent to England as candidate for commission.	
	19th		Divine Service at 9.30 a.m.	
	20th		Kit inspection. Training programme continued. 2 O.R. found. Working parties proceeded to wiring. At 8 p.m. "H" & "D" Coys employed carrying gas cylinders to front line.	
	21st		In morning training. In the afternoon a kit inspection was held and a revolver shooting competition for Officers. 1 O.R. S. WOODMEED admitted to Hospital. 1 O.R. joined. Working party proceeded to wiring.	
	22nd		MAJOR H.W. FESTING (15th D.L.I.) attached took over command of the Battalion. C.S. WAUGH. 1 O.R. wounded in ERVILLERS by anti-aircraft shell whilst on wiring party in BURG TRENCH. 3 O.R's joined.	
	23rd		1 O.R. wounded whilst on wiring party in BURG TRENCH. 3 O.R's joined.	
	24th		Training continued.	
			Training continued. Working parties proceeded as before. Divisional Concert Party at Coy. 3 O.R. joined.	2.
	25th		Training continued. Working parties were out as before. 1 Officer & 95 O.Rs sent to BERTRAUX-HU-MONT to cut sods.	

Army Form C. 2118.

WAR DIARY
or
INTELLIGENCE SUMMARY.
(Erase heading not required.)

Instructions regarding War Diaries and Intelligence Summaries are contained in F.S. Regs., Part II. and the Staff Manual respectively. Title pages will be prepared in manuscript.

Place	Date	Hour	Summary of Events and Information	Remarks and references to Appendices
BOISLEUX AU MONT	26th		Battalion moved from PATRICIA CAMP at 4 p.m. being relieved by the 1st MUNSTER REGT. and arriving at Camp (S.H.C.M.9) BOISLEUX-HU-MONT about 6 p.m.	
	27th		Draft of 73 O.R. joined at the above camp. Battalion marched from Camp at BOISLEUX-HU-MONT at 3 p.m. for BERNEVILLE. Draft of 29 O.R. joined the Battalion on the march. Very heavy rain during the whole march. Battalion arrived at BERNEVILLE about 6 p.m. Billets in Nissens.	
BERNEVILLE.	28th		Kit inspection of drafts.	
	29th		Inspection of Companies by Commanding Officer. Battalion being training in the morning. In the afternoon recreation. Brigade L.G. Examination.	
	30th		Training programme arranged.	
	31st		Training continued. The Brigadier General inspected drafts. A.G.C. & Divisional General inspected Camp & men at work.	

[signature]
Lt Col
Comdg R Dub Fus

WAR DIARY or INTELLIGENCE SUMMARY

Army Form C. 2118.

10th (S) BATTALION K.O.Y.L.I.
Date 2/10/17

Place	Date	Hour	Summary of Events and Information	Remarks and references to Appendices
BERNEVILLE	1917 Sept 1st		Training continued Attack formation practised in the afternoon and evening recreational training.	
	2nd 3rd		Battalion marched to SIMENCOURT to attend Brigade Church Parade. Training continued. Handling of arms Platoon drill sector drill continued and communication drill for Junior N.C.O.s and practised. Also musketry and bayonet training. Lewis Gun Officer 2nd Lieut Lewis started training. One Company firing on range Remainder - Musketry, Bombing and Bayonet training Rifles,	
	4th		Training continued. Vifles.	
	5th		2nd Lieut J.E. WOLSTENCROFT and two O.R. joined. Training continued. One Coy firing on range (50 Marks), Remainder - Platoon drill continued order drill (part done in afternoon and evening recreational Musketry and bayonet training in the afternoon and evening recreational Lewis.	
	6th		Training continued. One Company firing on range. Remainder - Company Drill, Platoon Drill Attack formation drill the musketry + bayonet training. In the afternoon and evening recreational training.	
	7th		Training continued. One Company firing on range. "H" + "C" Companies carried out Tactical Scheme. In the afternoon recreational training.	
	8th		Training continued. One Company on the range "B" + "D" Coys carried out tactical scheme in the afternoon Brigade Sports took place at SIMENCOURT.	
	9th		Battalion Church Parade.	
	10th		Training continued. "H" + "B" Coys carried out a march to Trench Attack.	
	11th		Battalion Field day Rifle Major St.C. + St.C.S.E. Battalion attacked as a Rifle Company frontage. "B" Coy + "D" Coys + "H" Coy in reserve. The School Idea was that the 64th Inf Bde. occupies the line from the Bois Grenier at R.8.C.8.5. to R.8.C.8.10.4. It had no Battalion by front line one in Support at R.8.a. and one in Reserve at BERNEVILLE. The 10th K.O.Y.L.I.	

WAR DIARY or INTELLIGENCE SUMMARY

Army Form C. 2118.

(Erase heading not required.)

Instructions regarding War Diaries and Intelligence Summaries are contained in F.S. Regs., Part II. and the Staff Manual respectively. Title pages will be prepared in manuscript.

Place	Date	Hour	Summary of Events and Information	Remarks and references to Appendices
BERNEVILLE	11th		was the right front Battalion. The 9th K.O.Y.L.I. on the 62nd Bde on our right. The Battalion objective was the area bounded by the lines joining the following co-ordinates :— R.14.c.6.9 to R.8.d.7.3 & R.15.a.3.5 & R.14.b.6.0. The attack was successfully carried out.	
	12th		In the afternoon Coats for the Officers of the Division were held at WAGONLIEU, Colonel PEETING presenting the big stick, event to the Officers of the Battalion. The Col. was 2nd Lt. BEAR being 2nd and the V.C. was "C" & "B" Coys. Training continued. "H" Company firing on the range. Captains carried out a march to Duisans. "B" Coy assault Practice. Musketry. Bayonet fighting and Bombing. In the afternoon 2nd Lieut HARRISON admitted to Hospital Training resumed. Having Profile.	
	13th		Brigade Field Day. This was carried out on the same lines as the Battalion Field Day, the 10th K.O.Y.L.I being the enemy.	
	14th		2nd Lieut. P.D. ROOKE and 4 O.R were sent in advance to CHELSTRE as billeting representatives. Training continued. D Company firing on the range. Remainder — Battalion drill. Extended order drill to two made bayonet fighting and musketry. In the evening the final of the Brigade Football Competition was played at SIMENCOURT Officers an evening game which ended in Battalion was beaten by the 10th K.O.Y.L.I by 5 goals to 2.	
	15th		In the morning the Battalion engaged cleaning up Camp etc. At 3 pm marched from BERNEVILLE to AUBIGNY arriving there at 6.15 p.m. and spent the night at billets.	
	16th		2nd Lt. H.C. WRABY admitted to Hospital. Reveille at 4.30 am. Battalion left AUBIGNY by train at 9.20 am for CASSELL.	
HENDEGHEM	17th		Arrived at CASSELL STATION at 2 pm and marched to BILLETS near HONDEGHEM, P.34.d.0.57. Battalion employed clearing up etc. 3 O.R. joined. At 11.30 pm 88 OR joined as reinforcements.	
	18th		Rest. March and Medical Inspection.	

A.5834 Wt. W.4973/M687 750,000 8/16 D.D. & L. Ltd. Forms/C.2118/13

Army Form C.2118.

WAR DIARY
or
INTELLIGENCE SUMMARY.
(Erase heading not required.)

Instructions regarding War Diaries and Intelligence Summaries are contained in F.S. Regs., Part II. and the Staff Manual respectively. Title pages will be prepared in manuscript.

Place	Date	Hour	Summary of Events and Information	Remarks and references to Appendices
HONDEGHEM	19th		Training continued. The whole Brigade practised an attack and carried aeroplanes.	
	20th		18 O.R. joined as reinforcement.	
	21st		Training continued under Company arrangements. "B" Coy Officers did Tactical Scheme with Brigadier General. In the afternoon recreational training.	
	22nd		Training continued under Coy arrangements. In the afternoon recreational training.	
	23rd		"ditto"	
			Marched from HONDEGHEM at 9am for THIEUSHOUK. Full Marching Order. Arrived at and departed at 12 noon. Battalion and Transport.	
THIEUSHOUK	24th		Reinforcement of 14 O.R. arrived. Battalion had received practically no training and quite unfit for the trenches. The morning was spent in Chasing up + carrying out Company arrangements.	
	25th	1 pm	Battalion paraded for inspection by Gen. Sir N.G.O. Plumer G.C.M.G. in command of 2nd Army. The General was able to attend and the Brigade was on the move. Training under Company arrangements and Companies proceeded to Baptism to look over SMETEREN Officers and NCO's practised the attack under the 22nd in command. Major F.B. BREWIS.	
	26th		Training in the Attack continued under Coy arrangements and recreational training in the late afternoon. A football match was played between Officers and Sergeants the latter winning by 3 goals to 2.	
	27th		Battalion practised the "Attack".	
			14 O.R. Reinforcements who arrived on the 24th inst proceeded to Depot Battalion. Bun football match was played between Officers and Sergeants the latter winning by 6 goals to 3. Battalion practised working up for attack. Bob Bogshots.	
	28th	6.30 pm	Battalion marched from THIEUSHOUK via BERTHEN and WESTOUTRE to CHIPPEWA CAMP, N.W. of LA CLYTTE (M.6.a.5.6) Ref. sheet 28/N.O.0.0	

Army Form C. 2118.

WAR DIARY
or
INTELLIGENCE SUMMARY.

(Erase heading not required.)

Instructions regarding War Diaries and Intelligence Summaries are contained in F. S. Regs., Part II. and the Staff Manual respectively. Title pages will be prepared in manuscript.

Place	Date	Hour	Summary of Events and Information	Remarks and references to Appendices
	29~		2nd Lieut JAMES and 5th O.R. proceeded YPRES as a working party. Battalion paraded for inoculation of Military Honors by (Bug. Ser. H.R. MENOLAM to:- 147811 Cpl. SYNES, M. 37629 L/Cpl SWINGLEHURST, J.V., 14501 Pte. SIDOLE, R.B., 13641 Pte. COWEN, C.	
	30~	9 am 11.30 am	The rest of the morning was spent in inspection by Coy. Comdr. E. Officers + N.C.O, practised the attack over a "flagged" course. Band Parade in Camp.	

1. 10. 17.

Alfred Cope M.D.
1st Lieut. Colonel.
Commanding 18th Bn. K.O.Y.L.I.

A 5834 Wt. W 4973/M687 750,000 8/16 D. D. & L. Ltd. Forms/C.2118/13

WAR DIARY or INTELLIGENCE SUMMARY

Army Form C.2118.

64/31

Place	Date	Hour	Summary of Events and Information	Remarks and references to Appendices
LA CLYTTE	1/10/17		The Battalion paraded and left CHIPPEWA CAMP (Sheet 28 - N.6 central) (Map Ko4c1) proceeding to SCOTTISH WOOD. (Sheet 28.- H.35.d), East of DICKEBUSCH LAKE. The nucleus party (or rather the remnants of it) were left behind at CHIPPEWA CAMP. The thought going to an officer and WILTSHIRE FARM, S.W. of SCOTTISH WOOD. One party of 50 men and an Officer had already left the Nucleus party and gone away to build a Brigade H.Q. in STIRLING CASTLE (J.13). This party were later employed in Lewin Beam work. SCOTTISH WOOD was not a very comfortable camp. Owing to the employment habits of bombing in which the enemy frequently indulges in this part of the world the huts and bivouacs have got to have sandbags round them to the height of about three feet, or else the ground inside the huts has to be dug-out The result is that in wet weather the shelters and huts are simply full of water. However as we had only one night to spend there the men worried much and everyone settled in for a good long night. This however was rudely disturbed by orders from Division that we were to move off at 2 hours notice & relieve the 9th Br. K.O.Y.L.I. in ZILLEBEKE Railway Embankment. Owing to the enemy having attacked the 110th Bde very heavily in the afternoon and caused casualties the 9th K.O.Y.L.I. had been hurriedly moved up into close support at CLAPHAM JUNCTION. The consequence was that leaving the move made take place, the early part of the night was spent in issuing bombs, flares, extra ammunition etc. However we did not move, and a quiet night was spent about.	
SCOTTISH WOOD	Oct 2		The morning was spent in issuing Operation Orders and in going into the exact details of the attack, and in putting the finishing touch to the preparations. All packs were dumped with the Quartermaster at WILTSHIRE FARM.	

Army Form C.118.

WAR DIARY
or
INTELLIGENCE SUMMARY.
(Erase heading not required.)

Instructions regarding War Diaries and Intelligence Summaries are contained in F.S. Regs., Part II. and the Staff Manual respectively. Title pages will be prepared in manuscript.

Place	Date	Hour	Summary of Events and Information	Remarks and references to Appendices
SCOTTISH WOOD	Oct 2nd		The Battalion paraded at 4.15 p.m., and marched to the Railway Embankment (I.21.c.4.6) S.W. of ZILLEBEKE LAKE where they occupied dug-outs. "D" Coy under Lieut. BARRETT were detached from the Battalion and came under the Command of the O.C. 15th D.L.I.	
	Oct 3rd		The day was spent quietly, everyone resting and preparing themselves for the great events that were to come off on the next day.	
			The Battalion paraded at 11 p.m. and marched off to the assembly positions for an account of these operations see appendix "A" attd.	
	Thurs Oct 4th Fri " 5th Sat " 6th " 1/2		The Battalion, wet, footsore and very weary arrived back at the embankment at about 4.30 a.m. Excellent arrangements had been made and everything was ready for the men when they came in. They were first of all given a drink of tea and rum after which there was soup and stew for them. Cigarettes were distributed free and every man was issued with an overcoat. Soap and towels had also been brought up so that every man could get a wash. The rest of the morning was spent in a well earned sleep. In the afternoon the Batt. (now about 150 strong) marched back to SCOTTISH WOOD, where the night was spent.	
ZILLEBEKE RAILWAY EMBANKMENT				
	Monday Oct. 8th		At 4.30 p.m. the Battalion marched to entrain at OUDGEROM. The weather party joined in at the Station. It was an appallingly wet night, and very uncomfortable for everyone. We arrived at the Station at 6.30 p.m. The train	

A.5834 Wt.W4973/M687 750,000 8/16 D.D. & L. Ltd. Forms/C.2118/13

WAR DIARY
or
INTELLIGENCE SUMMARY.

(Erase heading not required.)

Army Form C.2118.

Place	Date	Hour	Summary of Events and Information	Remarks and references to Appendices
	Oct 8		being due to leave at 7.40 p.m. It did not, however, leave until 9.45 p.m. and during the whole of the three hours the Battalion was standing out in the pouring rain getting colder and colder. We eventually steamed out of OUDEZEEDOM about 10 p.m. and arrived at EBBLINGHEM about 3 a.m.	
	Oct 9th, 10th, 11th		For the next two days the Battalion was engaged in cleaning up, reorganising and generally endeavouring to get back to normal routine. Casualty lists were compared. The figures were found to be as follows. Killed 4 Officers 29 O.R. wounded 4, 241. missing 2, 40.	
	Oct 12th		A very large number of the wounded were very light and not were walking cases. The Brigadier General came and gave a short congratulatory address to the Battalion. He reminded them that this was the third time on which the 61st Brigade had been left and its Right Flank in the air, the former occasions being (1) Attack at FRICOURT on the 1st July 1916, (2) Attack on HINDENBURG LINE on April 9th.	
	Oct 13		The remainder of the morning was spent in bathing the men. A route march had been planned, but owing to the bad weather it was postponed, and parades were carried out under Coy arrangements.	
	Oct 14 Oct 15		Church Parade services were held in the morning the rest of the day was a holiday. During the morning some Coys went to baths, others carried on Coy Parades.	

WAR DIARY or INTELLIGENCE SUMMARY

Army Form C.2118.

(Erase heading not required.)

Place	Date	Hour	Summary of Events and Information	Remarks and references to Appendices
	October			
	16.		During the afternoon sports were held for the benefit of the transport. The events being (1) Whimsical Chair (2) for mules (3) for draughts (C) for H.Draughts. (2) Pig-sticking on mules (3) Wrestling on horseback. The whole show was got up on very short notice, but was quite a success.	
	17.		The route march postponed from 13th was carried out. The G.O.C. Division was met on the road. He watched the men march by him, and said that they ought to be exceedingly proud of themselves.	
	18th 19th 20th		Company training was continued. Special attention being paid to Lewis Gun tactics, bayonet fighting and musketry. He was been slung - there is no doubt that the Battalion has been very lucky compared with many others in the Division who have been sent up road-making. Company training and general reorganisation. Every Company was marched into two platoons.	
	21st		The Battalion moved by train back to BREWERY CAMP, out of DICKEBUSCH. The Battalion arrived about midday and found that the Camp contained about 50 tents which floated on a sea of mud. However it was known that we were only there for one night, and everyone settled down to make the best of it.	
	23rd		The Battalion moved in the early afternoon to Railway Dugouts at ZILLEBEKE where they relieved the 9th K.O.Y.L.I. The Battalion moved off in early afternoon to take over the left sector of the Brigade relieving 15th D.L.I. This extended from REUTER CEMETERY on the right to about 800 yards to the N.E. of the Cemetery. On the way up the shelling beyond HOOGE CRATER was somewhat heavy, one shell falling right in the middle of "B" Company.	

WAR DIARY
or
INTELLIGENCE SUMMARY.
(Erase heading not required.)

Army Form C.118.

Place	Date	Hour	Summary of Events and Information	Remarks and references to Appendices
	23rd		The result was that our casualties whilst going in amounted to about 20, including 2nd Lieuts FOX & DRAPER and C.S.M. CLETHRO. All three last three belonged to "C" Coy, 2nd Lt FOX being in charge of the Coy. In consequence 2nd Lt DORE was told to take over command of "C" Coy temporarily. The disposition in the line was, "B" Coy on the right front, "A" Coy on the left front, and "C" & "D" were in support. Relief was reported complete at 11.30 p.m., but this was not really correct as 2nd Lt ROOKE and half "B" Coy were led astray by their guide & eventually found themselves with the left flank Coy of the 9th Yorks who were in the Battalion's right. He tried to get his troop with his own Coy who were on his left but failed to do so and did not succeed in joining them until two nights later.	OFFICERS K.W.M. 2 — OTHER RANKS K. W. M. 2 12 0
	24th		During the early morning the shelling of "D" Coy in support was very heavy and caused several casualties. It was found that communication by day was not easy as beyond half way there was no track of any kind marked. By night communication at first was practically impossible. There was a good deal of shelling at intervals during	1 — 5 14 4
	25th		the day, and some sniping on both sides. At other times it was very quiet, and the enemy were undoubtedly afraid lest we should attack, and every day at dawn and dusk he used to put down a protectiv barrage. In order to avoid further casualties to the support Coys one third of the two Companies was moved to the support line joining "B" Coy, one third was sent back to the BUTTE, the remainder staying where they were. This disposition was only	6

WAR DIARY or INTELLIGENCE SUMMARY.

Army Form C. 2118.

Place	Date	Hour	Summary of Events and Information	Remarks and references to Appendices
				OFFICERS K W M / **OTHER RANKS** K W M
	25th		adopted when it was known that an enemy barrage was likely	
	26th		At 5.40 a.m. an advance was made on the right of the Division and to the left, but on the actual Divisional front an attack was merely simulated by a creeping barrage. On the left the attack by the Canadians was a complete success. On the right the Seventh Div. failed to take GHELUVELT and the 5th Division although they actually took POLDERHOEK CHATEAU, evacuated it later in the day owing to their right flank being in the air. This attack naturally brought down an enemy barrage upon our lines but this was not so much damage as might have been expected. During the afternoon a track to the front line was marked by means of stakes. Most of the day rain fell heavily, making the conditions in the front line extremely bad.	1 5 2
	27th		The day was spent fairly quietly and in the evening the Battalion was relieved by the 9th Lincoln Reg't. The relief was carried out with complete success, and two Coys. ("A" v "B") went down to CLAPHAM JUNCTION for the night while "C" & "D" stayed in support near POLYGONE BUTTE	8
	28th		"A" & "B" Coys. now moved to ZILLEBEKE EMBANKMENT and from there on to BREWERY CAMP. "C" & "D" Coys came out and were the night at ZILLEBEKE EMBANKMENT. Our total casualties for these 6 days were =	2
	29th		"C" & "D" Coys. joined the rest of the Battalion at BREWERY CAMP. The day was spent endeavouring to restore cleanliness. The men were chiefly troubled with bad feet. The rain of the 26th had made the feet	3 / 8 48 6

WAR DIARY
or
INTELLIGENCE SUMMARY.
(Erase heading not required.)

Army Form C.118.

Instructions regarding War Diaries and Intelligence Summaries are contained in F. S. Regs., Part II. and the Staff Manual respectively. Title pages will be prepared in manuscript.

Place	Date	Hour	Summary of Events and Information	Remarks and references to Appendices
	31st		well, & when boots were taken off it was found difficult to get them on again. However the number of cases of trench feet was fewer than was originally expected. "C" Coy (under Lt WALTER) moved up again as a Support Coy for the Right Battalion of the left Brigade. Their position is now the POLYGONE BUTTE.	

L.A. Thurn
Capt. A.S.M.
for K.O.Y.L.I.

10th (S) Bn. King's Own Yorkshire Light Infantry.

From: BITS   to TIN.   (M.294)   3/10/17.

      Owing to heavy casualties to-day, 15th D.L.I. are unable to carry out task aaa 1st E. Yorks. R. will take 2nd Objective and form up immediately behind 9th K.O.Y.L.I. aaa 10th K.O.Y.L.I. will place one Coy at disposal of 1st E. York. R. to support attack. aaa Coy of 10th K.O.Y.L.I. now with 15th Durh. L.I. will reform and be in reserve. aaa Lt. Col. BEYTS will assist Lt. Col. WAITHMAN in every way possible aaa In event of 1st E. York. R. having to assist 9th K.O.Y.L.I. to take 1st Objective, O.C. 10th K.O.Y.L.I. will support E. York R. to take 2nd Objective with 1 or 2 more Coys as asked for by 1st E. York. R. aaa Action of the 4 M.Gs will be the same with the 1st E. York. R. as it was to have been with 15th Durh. L. I.

10.15p.m.   (signed) A.F. MACDOUGALL, Major.

From: BITS   to TIN   (M.276)   3/10/17.

      Ref. M.294 TIN will take 2nd Objective and not BRASS aaa BRASS will be in support and act as originally ordered for TIN in Brigade O.O. para 8 (c) aaa Silver is responsible that Coy TIN at present with SILVER joins TIN on TINS way to assembly.

11.30 p.m.   (signed) A.F. MACDOUGALL, Major.

From: BITS   to: TIN   (M.290)   4/10/17.

      If 10th K.O.Y.L.I. is drawn into fighting for 1st Objective and unfit to advance to 2nd Objective East Yorks will take 2nd Objective. In this case O.C. 10th must inform O.C. E.Y. at once so that E.Y. can form up. O.C. 10th will reorganise and push forward a Company in support of E.Y. in its attack on 2nd Objective. Acknowledge. - Adressed TIN and BRASS.

12.30 a.m.   (signed)   H. R. HEADLAM. B.G. BITS.

From: Sigs BITS   to: TIN   (H.42)   4/10/17.

Messages for Bde. to BLACK WATCH CORNER - PILL BOX Thence by lamp to FITZCLARENCE FARM aaa No line possible as yet aaa Cpl ROADHOUSE i/c of B. WATCH STATION.

9 a.m.

(2)

From: TIN   to: BITS   (O.R.6)   4/10/17.

TIN ready in position aaa One Company BRASS has reported and is in position aaa Two more Companies BRASS are in position behind me aaa BRASS and TIN Hd. Qrs at JERK FARM at J.15.b.7.8.

4.50 a.m.   (signed) H.W. FESTING, Lt. Col.

From: TIN   to: IRON   (O.R.7)   4/10/17

My Battalion is in position about 40 yards behind yours aaa They will advance at ZERO and will capture second Objective aaa They have orders to assist you in attack on first Objective if required aaa My Hd. Qrs. is at JERK FARM J.15.b.7.8. BRASS Hd. Qrs. is with me and I have one Coy BRASS in support of me and there are two more Companies in rear of me with orders to advance when first Objective is captured and dig in facing South East west of POLYGONE BEEK aaa

5.15 a.m.   (signed) J. MAGIN, 2nd/Lt.

From: O.C. "B" Coy   to: TIN   4/10/17.

Have consolidated aaa The 1st LINCOLNS are on my left aaa Have reported to C.O. IRON aaa Capt. MARSH appears to be overlapping my front.

5.20 a.m.   (signed) F.D. ROOKE, 2nd/Lt.

From: TIN   to BITS   (O.R.8)   4/10/17.

Situation obscure aaa Troops have been seen moving on the 1st Objective aaa It is uncertain whether these are our men or the enemy aaa No reports received from Companies yet aaa A few prisoners have been seen passing down aaa

7.15 a.m.   (JERK FARM) (signed) L.D. SPICER, Capt & Adjt.

From: TIN   to BITS   (O.R.9)   4/10/17

Wounded report that 1st Objective is captured aaa About 60 prisoners have been passed down the line aaa No reports from Companies yet aaa Wounded also report that TIN are formed up at the 1st Objective ready to advance when barrage lifts aaa This is unconfirmed aaa

7.35 a.m.   (signed) L. D. SPICER, Capt & Adjt

From TIN   to BITS   (O.R.10)   4/10/17

No further messages yet received from the front line aaa Situation obscure aaa Officer has been sent forward to reconnoitre aaa

9.55 a.m.   (signed) H.W. FESTING Lt. Col.

From: Sigs.BITS   to TIN   (H.46)   4/10/17

From Objective there is good chance for your visual stations to gather in news and send it back to you or FITZCLARENCE FARM.

10.25 a.m.

(3)

From: Sigs BITS   to TIN (H.40)   4/10/17

Please detail visual Party to take up positions suitable
for gathering news from all your front and will transmit
to B.W. CORNER, where Brigade Party will be stationed to
receive and distribute aaa It may suit position of station
chosen, please forward to B.W. Corner.

11/10 am.

From: O. C. "A" COY   to TIN   4/10/17

Am at present holding and consolidating a line in front
of 1st Objective.   The line is fairly well held, 9th Bn,
East Yorks and B.V.L.I. 10th K.O.Y.L.I.   I have got one
reserve Lewis Gun which you sent up here and one or two
others. I have posts out in front and an Officer of the
12th 13th N.Fs is holding a support line in rear about 100
yards.
        I don't think there are any other 10th Officers
up here, but Capt. FRANKS, 10th East Yorks, is here. I have
got quite a decent number of "A" Coy men with me.
        I am not yet quite sure where my right is on the
map.

9 p.m. ?   (signed) A. MEIN, Captain,

From TIN   to BITS (O.R.12) 4/10/17

Our troops can be seen on ridge at 1st Objective aaa Have
not gained touch with my Coys yet aaa Officer despatched
with Orderly to get into touch, at 9.30 a.m., has not
returned aaa Heavy enemy barrage on my Headquarters apparently coming from East by South.

1.15 p.m.   (signed) H. W. FESTING, Lt. Col.

From O.C. "A" Coy   to   TIN   4/10/17.

Enemy counter-attacking our present line and heavily shelling.
We have a defensive flank ready to meet him at J.11.c.6.5.

2.30 p.m.   (signed) A. MEIN, Captain,

From: 2nd/Lt J.W. DORE   to: TIN   4/10/17.

Enemy counter-attacking present position (J.11.c.6.5.). aaa
Am staying in present position until enemy action is over.

2.42 p.m.   (signed) J. W. DORE, 2nd/Lieut.

From: TIN   to: BITS (O.R.14) 4/10/17

Enemy reported to have worked round between right of 64th
Brigade and left of the 5th Division aaa I am uncertain in
whose possession JUT FARM J.16.a.3.1. now is aaa Officers
patrol being sent there to-night aaa

5.23 p.m.   (signed) H. W. FESTING, Lt. Col.

(4)

From: TIN   to: O.C. Div'l Dump   (O.R.15)   4/10/17.

Please issue bearer with 12 S.O.S. Rifle Grenades aaa URGENT.

5.35 p.m.   (signed) L. D. SPICER, Capt & Adjt.

From: TIN   to BITS, (O.R.16)   4/10/17.

Two Officers just returned from front line report as follows aaa First Objective is held by mixed body of troops from the Division aaa East Yorks and others are dug in on the line of the road from J.11.c.40.35 - J.11.c.40.00 aaa About a Coy of D.L.I. are dug in along the line of the road J.11.b.3.9. (approx) facing S.E. aaa Our Machine Guns appear to be about 200 yards North of the D.L.I. firing East (approx).aaa Owing to the mingling of Units it is impossible to estimate casualties aaa There appear to be sufficient Officers and men to hold the line for to-night aaa One Officer reports that enemy appear to be working round right flank of this (21st)Division} aaa CAMERON COVERT appears to be the danger spot. aaa

6.50 p.m.   (signed) H. W. FESTING, Lt. Col.

From: BRASS   to BITS (O.R.17)   4/10/17

Reserve in hands of TIN and BRASS totals about 18 O.R. aaa Troops immediately in front and on right flank have been very severely shelled at least four times to-day aaa Am endeavouring to ascertain the exact situation but consider one fresh Battalion in reserve advisable as soon as possible aaa

            (signed) R.H. WRAITHMAN, Lt. Col.

From: BITS   to   TIN (M.15)   4/10/17.

The Germans are trying to break through on our right flank up the POLYGONE BEEK aaa 15th D.L.I. ordered to JOIST FARM and road line just West of it aaa 15th D.L.I. ordered to push strong patrols to POLYGONe BEEK and deal with Germans aaa 95th Inf. Bde. has reserves in CAMERON COVERT and are ordering these forward aaa Endeavour to organise the line and get some men in reserve especially about cottages in J.11.c.0.5 aaa Have you any men in REUTEL aaa Your cypher message indecipherable aaa Use B.A.B. Code or plain aaa ANZACS & VII Division stated to have got all objectives aaa
7.45 p.m.   (signed) H. R. HEADLAM, Brigadier.

From: BITS   to   TIN   (X.Y.20)   4/10/17

Herewith 1 box S.O.S. Rockets and two daylight Mortar Signals. That is all there is at Brigade Headquarters. There are none at Divisional Dump, where I found your Orderly with the request. Please give ½ these signals to BRASS as they also want some. Also 1 box of S.O.S. Rifle Grenades was sent up with each Battalions rations to-day. Rations left CLAPHAM JUNCTION on mules O.K. 6r both Battalions at about 6 p.m. with orders to go to your Headquarters at JERK HOUSE.

8 p.m.   (signed) H. LEE, Staff Captain.

From: Corps via BITS to TIN   4/10/17.

Water supply J.17.a.9.7. near JUNIPER COTTAGE. Water flowing into pond abundant and good. Wells J.11.c.1.3. South of the road near the houses - water good and plentiful.
When there is one large house standing alone usually a well outside the house a few yards away from back wall of house. When a group of houses, well usually behind centre house two or three yards from back wall.
Wells are not open but formed by natural springs flowing into a brick vault covered by about 8' of earth.
Wells 5 to 6 metres deep and 1 metre to 1.20 in diameter. Well water usually very good.

From: O.C. "B" Coy   to TIN   5/10/17.

Have taken all messages aaa Will deliver to other Coys as soon as possible aaa Will carry out all instructions at my earliest convenience aaa

4.0. a.m.   (signed) P. D. ROOKE, 2nd/Lt.

From: TIN   to SIGS BITS   (J.M.17) 5/10/17

Advanced Station still working aaa Iron Signals joining me and will organise. We have sufficient lamps aaa One is fixed on your Headquarters (FITZCLARENCE FARM) and many messages already sent aaa Up to now all messages sent to you by lamp have also been sent by runners for safety aaa We have no P.B. and IRONS has been blown up aaa

4.35 a.m.   (signed) J. MAGIN, 2nd/Lt.

From: TIN   to BITS   (O.R. 19) 5/10/17

Have just returned from reconnoitring front line and can report as follows aaa SILVER hold the line of the road J.11.b.05.90 to J.11.b.90.50 (aporox) facing S by E, with one Company LEICESTERS on their left holding the line of trench J.11.b.80.30 to J.10.b.55.10 (aporox) facing S.E. aaa SILVER reports that he is in touch with 5th Division on the right aaa IRON and TIN hold the line of JUDGE TRENCH from J.11.c.40.50 to the road at J.11.c.40.30 aaa BRASS holds from J.11.c.40.27 to J.11.c.20.10. aaa Two Vickers Machine Guns are in position on the above line immediately North and South of the road aaa 12/13 N.Fs, strength uncertain, hold the line of the road from J.11.c.50.50 to J.11.c.30.10 aaa Units are reorganising aaa O.C. Coys have received orders to form local reserves aaa From personal observation the line on the left of this Brigade appears to be scattered but men can be seen along the Ridge aaa My Battalion strength appears to be not more than 100 rifles at present aaa S.O.S. was sent up this morning about 5.30 a.m. by a small party about 200 yards East of our present forward posts aaa Details concerning this party are at present unknown but instructions have been issued to get in touch with them aaa CAMERON COVER is still held by enemy and is a commanding position on our right flank aaa Enemy M.Gs from this point cover the road approaching our front line aaa Enemy yesterday massed behind CAMERON COVER for Counter - Attack and this point can clearly be seen from our forward posts and fire was brought to bear on the enemy by shooting over our own parados aaa Two enemy aeroplanes were flying low over our forward line about

8330 a.m. this morning aaa At present I have three Officers in the front line, three at my Bn. H.Q., exclusive of my Signal Officer, Adjutant and myself aaa Details as to Officer casualties as far as known will be forwarded forthwith.

10. 0. a.m.   (signed) H. W. FESTING, Lt. Colonel.

From: TIN to Capt. DAY, IRON, (O.R.37)   5/10/17.

Please try and get in touch before dawn with that unknown post reported to be about 150 yards in front of your line aaa Also please send out a small patrol through REUTEL and find out (1) How far forward are our furthest posts in REUTEL (2) Whether enemy has any posts in REUTEL aaa

12.30 p.m.   (signed) L. D. SPICER, Capt. & Adjt.

From: TIN to Capt. DAY, IRON (O.R.38)   5/10/17.

Brigade wire reads:- You will probably be relieved to-morrow night (6/7th), either by Our own Nucleous or by another unit. aaa What ho !!!

12.30 p.m.   (signed) L. D. SPICER, Capt. & Adjt.

From: TIN to BITS   (O.R.20)   5/10/17.

Reference my O.R. 19 in Map Reference for left of SILVER and right of PALM read J.16.b.50.90 for J.16.b.90.50 aaa Silver now report that their line runs from J.16.a.5.7. to J.16.b.9.9.

1.0. p.m.   (signed) L. D. SPICER, Capt. & Adjt.

From : BITS to : TIN (B.M.611)   5/10/17.

All captured German Machine Guns are to be sufficiently destroyed so as to be out of action aaa

3.15 p.m.   (signed) A.F. MACDOUGALL, Bde. Major,

From: TIN to O. C. IRON COY (O.R.25)   5/10/17.

Please have guides at J.10.d.9.1. (on road) at 9 p.m.

5.10 p.m.   (signed) J. MAGIN, 2nd/Lt.

From: TIN to Captain DAY, IRON (O.R.30)   5/10/17.

All captured German Machine Guns are to be sufficiently destroyed so as to be out of action aaa

6.5. p.m.   (signed) J. MAGIN, 2nd/Lt.

From : BITS to TIN (M.28)   5/10/17.

Ref. M. 25, 5th Division has now been ordered to Consolidate with left at Bridge J.10.d.8.1. and right on REUTEL BEEK J.16.b.3.0. aaa When this move is completed and 5th Division left consolidates on Objective SILVER will move across the POLYGONE BEEK and consolidate line of road from left of 5th Division to JUNIPER TRENCH, J.11.c.1.4. as a Support Line aaa TIN is to reconnoitre REUTEL as from reports received we have posts in Village and enemy have not.

From 6.25 p.m.   (signed) A.F. MACDOUGALL, Bde. Major,

(7a) to be inserted in 7 at @

FROM : TIN   to : BITS   (O.R.40)   6/10/17

2nd/Lt DORE took out a small patrol between 2 a.m. and 2.30 this morning to find out (1) whether we had any isolated posts in REUTEL (2) If the enemy had any posts in REUTEL aaa He reports that (1) We have no posts beyond the line of posts from J.11.c.6.3. to J.11.c.6.5. which form our front line (2) The enemy has no Posts in REUTEL. aaa The situation during the night has been as follows :- S.O.S. twice signalled by our front line and once by the enemy aaa Heavy barrage apparently to the North commenced at 6 a.m. and lasted about ½ hour aaa Very Heavy Enemy shelling in the vicinity of BLACK-WATCH CORNER and JERK HOUSE aaa Reference my former report re strongpoint occupied by enemy on right flank of Bde. front, this was reported to you to be CAMERON COVERT it however now appears that the S.P. is situated at POLDERHOEK CHATEAU J.16.d.2.2.
                                           (signed) L. D. SPICER, Capt & Adjt.

From : TIN   to Medical Officer   (O.R. 42)   6/10/17.

Attached report from 2nd/Lt. DORE is forwarded to you, Please try and send some up if you possibly can we have sent you all the men we can possibly spare aaa If your stretcher bearers do not know the way tell them to come here and I will send them on with guides aaa No stretcher bearers have actually been to the front line aaa

9.30. a.m.   (signed) L. D. SPICER, Capt & Adjt.

(7)

From : TIN   to Regt'l Aid Post (O.R.36)   5/10/17.

Bearer is in charge of three other men told off to assist you in stretcher bearing.

9.55 p.m.   (signed) J. MAGIN, 2nd/Lieut.

From: 2nd/Lt J.W. DORE to TIN   (information) 6.10.17.

Enemy twice caught massing troops for counter-attack but each time destroyed by barrage fire. aaa   Enemy signals- One Green - Retaliation, One yellow bursting into a series of yellow lights - Artillery Firing Short., Two Reds - S.O.S., Two Whites - Reinforce aaa.

12.20 a.m.   (signed) J. W. DORE, 2nd/Lieut.

From: 2nd/Lieut J.W. DORE to TIN   6/10/17.

Received one small jar of rum by runner. Thanks very much for same aaa Could you by any chance get some white very Lights and send same up as soon as possible. aaa Situation All quiet at present aaa

12.26 a.m.   (signed) J. W. DORE, 2nd/Lieut.

From : 2nd/Lt. J. W. DORE, to TIN (Patrol Report) 6/10/17.

Strength - 1 Offr and 4 other ranks. Offr in charge 2nd/Lt. J. W. DORE.   Object - Find out if enemy occupied any part of REUTEL and positions of our advanced posts aaa Patrol pushed up road from J.11.c.7.25 to J.11.d.2.6. at the same time searching village which was found to be unoccupied. aaa On return came by route on O.T., J.11.O.2.6. to J.11. c. 85.45 via J.11.c.75.65. All these were found to be unoccupied. aaa From personal opinion present line could be pushed forward for another 200 yards aaa Nothing was seen of Advanced Post that was reported to be isolated aaa

4.36 a.m.   (signed) J. W. DORE, 2nd/Lieut.

From : 2nd/Lt DORE, J.W. to TIN (Situation Report) 6/10/17.

Situation - All quiet aaa Have got plenty of S.A.A. aaa We have received rations from 9th Bn. there are plenty of them but no rations for 10th have turned up yet aaa.

5.35 a.m.   (signed) J. W. DORE, 2nd/Lieut.

insert 7a

From : Capt. Day IRON to TIN   6/10/17.

Our artillery are shelling our own trenches and have been doing so all night aaa They have already knocked out two men aaa It is enfilade fire on to the right i.e. SOUTH of REUTEL aaa All our artillery are shortening their range aaa It is certain that they were not acquainted with the position of our Infantry. aaa Can this be rectified aaa

11.5 a.m.   (signed) A. DAY, Captain, IRON.

From : Captain BRYCER TIN to Capt DAY IRON (I.S.2) 6/10/17.

Reference artillery shooting short this has already been reported to Corps by Aircon twice and a report has also been sent to bde.

another urgent message is in process of being sent now by
lamp and by runner to Bde. aaa I am very sorry you are still
being bothered but I do not know what else we can do aaa

11.42 a.m.   (signed) L. D. SPICER, Capt & Adjt.

From : BITS TIN   to BITS   (O.R.39)   6/10/17.

Front Line report enemy twice caught massing troops for
counter attack to-night but each time attack was destroyed
by barrage fire aaa Enemy Light Signals appear to be as
follows : 2 reds - S.O.S., 1 green - Retaliation, 1
yellow bursting into yellow rain - Artillery lengthen
range, 2 Whites - reinforce ?

1.15 p.m.   (signed) L. D. SPICER, Capt. & Adjt.

From : 2nd/Lt A. WALTER to TIN (A.W.1) 6/10/17.

Brigade H.Q. have made arrangements for Guides to meet the
relief at CLAPHAM JUNCTION aaa As far as I can gather they
are two Coys of Leicesters who are going to take over front
line aaa The parties of 9th and 10th will be with them and
will be in support. aaa The Brigadier will not let me wait
to guide them and directs me to go on to Transport Lines aaa
I shall go on to Embankment and do what I can there until
you arrive aaa

3.40 p.m.   (signed) A. WALTER, 2nd/Lieut.

From TIN   to Captain DAY, IRON (S.F. 3)   6/10/17

On relief all men of other Units attached to you will come
out with you aaa They will march under your orders down to
the ZILLEBEKE Railway Embankment and will stop with your
men for the night aaa If possible get a nominal roll of them
made out aaa Further instructions regarding the disposal
of these men will be issued to-morrow aaa Please warn all
ranks under your command to make sure that they come out
properly and fully equipped aaa

5.45 p.m.   (signed) L. D. SPICER, Capt. & Adjt.

Certified that the above are true copies
of messages sent & received between Oct 3rd & 6th 1917

L. D. Spicer
Captain & Adjutant,
10th (S) Bn. K. O. Yorkshire L. I.

10th (S) Bn. K. O. Yorkshire L. I.

October 11th 1917.

The 10th K.O.Y.L.I. left the Railway Embankment at ZILLEBEKE at 11 p.m., October 3rd to march up into position.

On the way up orders were received from Brigade that the original plan of attack had been altered and that, owing to the 15th D.L.I. having received many casualties from Shell Fire, the 10th K.O.Y.L.I. would take the 2nd Objective, the 1st East Yorkshire Reg't should support their attack and the 15th D.L.I. would be in Brigade Reserve.

Despite Enemy Shell Fire the march up as far as CLAPHAM JUNCTION was without casualties and the men kept exceedingly well closed up. At CLAPHAM JUNCTION the Battalion picked up four guides who had been up to reconnoitre the route. The guides, however, were of little use and they all four managed to lose their way within 300 yards. Fortunately one Officer and one N.C.O. per Company had been sent up in the afternoon and with assistance from them the Battalion safely arrived at BLACKWATCH CORNER. From their it was not far to the forming up tape which had been laid out previously that night. Owing to the alteration in plans the tape was too far back for actual forming up but was extremely useful in giving direction. By 4.30 a.m. October 4th all the Companies had been shewn their places and by 5.30 a.m. they were properly in position. Headquarters had been established in a small MEBUS about 14 feet long 8 feet broad and 5 feet high. It was one of a colony of 5 or 6 MEBUS, which obviously had formerly formed an enemy strongpoint. The 1st East Yorkshire Reg't being unable to find any other Headquarters were offered room and established in the same place.

The disposition of Companies for the attack was as follows:-

"C" Coy   -   right Front Coy.
"B" "   -   left   "   "
"D" "   -   right Support Coy.
"A" "   -   left   "   "

At 6 a.m. (zero hour) the Battalion moved off close on the heels of the 9th Bn. K.O.Y.L.I. After going a short distance the right Companies, both of the 9th and 10th Battns were held up by a strongpoint (a machine gun in a defended shell hole). An attack was being organised on this point with rifle grenadiers when a tank appeared close behind the right Coy and the enemy surrendered. This strongpoint did not affect the left Companies who went straight on down into the POLYGONE BEEK VALLEY. The 9th and 10th K.O.Y.L.I. became mixed up on the right owing to the delay caused by the strongpoint. On arrival at the BEEK owing to the marshy nature of the ground, direction became somewhat lost and though some Officers and men crossed the BEEK by means of tree trunks etc., a large number of men converged on to the road on the right. During the crossing of the BEEKE heavy rifle and machine gun fire was experienced coming apparently from the right flank, from the direction of JUNIPER WOOD. At this period a good many of the casualties occurred and both Battalions became mixed all along the line. The time was now about 6.30 or 6.45 a.m.

A strongish belt of wire held up the right front Coy when they came to JOIST FARM (J.10.d.2.2.), but those who had gone round by the road avoided this wire. When the tanks came up they broke the belt of wire through which 2nd/Lt. ROOKE of "B" Coy with his men went forward. After the tanks had gone through the Germans were surrendering in parties and some delay was caused to leading Companies, particularly the right front Coy, in clearing up the ground and sending back prisoners.

The advance then proceeded smoothly but the line had become very much mixed up and somewhat thinned owing to casualties. Little resistance was met with going up the hill from the valley and the leading men of the 9th and 10th K.O.Y.L.I. arrived at the 1st Objective together. On reaching the 1st Objective a party of some 30 N.Fs under an Officer appeared just on the left of the REUTEL ROAD (J.16.b.1.9. - J.11.d.2.3.), and joined the right rear Coy. Small parties of Devons, D.C.L.I., and Queens were also mixed up with the Battalion on the 1st Objective.

The right front Coy did not arrive at the 1st Objectiv until the barrage had already started moving forward toward the 2nd Objective. The reasons for the delay were:-
(1) They were held up by wire in the valley,(presumably in front of JOIST FARM).
(2) They had difficulty in crossing POLYGONE BEEK.
(3) They were employed for some time in clearing up the ground and sending back prisoners.

In consequence the right support Coy which had gone by the road arrived at the 1st Objective considerably before the right front Coy.

During the hour and 40 minutes (standing barrage beyond the 1st Objective) the right of the Battalion was chiefly employed in cleaning up the ground and turning the enemy out of Shell Holes etc. The left was lying behind the 1st Objective, mixed up with the 9th Battalion and was heavily shelled.

It appears that all the Officers of the Right Support Coy and all the Officers of the right Front Coy were killed or wounded by rifle and machine gun fire from JOIST FARM. On reaching the 1st Objective there were only two Officers in the Battalion left.

When the barrage lifted remnants of the Battalion, particularly on the left, worked forward for about 200 yards or so, but owing to the fact that the Battalion had had many casualties both to Officers and men previous to this, and that a certain number were employed making a defensive right flank, there was not more than 50 men available to go forward, some of whom were from other Units.

On arrival at the 1st Objective the Officer on the spo states that he could see none of the Division on our right, which should have been up level with him and being anxious about his right flank he decided that after advancing 150 yards from the 1st Objective it was impossible to hold a longer right flank without endangering the whole line. He therefore collected such men as he could and formed a defensive flank. The line never got farther forward than this. (J.11.c.8.3. - J.11.c.6.2. - J.11.a.4.1.).

During the afternoon in the short intervals when the enemy was not shelling the front trenches the troops in the front line could do little but make a certain amount of cover, by connecting shell holes. When night fell the two Officers and two Coy Sergeant Majors who were in command dug their trenches at a line North of REUTEL, facing East. This trench was continued by the 9th Bn. as far as the road which runs through REUTEL. On the South of the road some men of the 1st East Yorkshire Reg't under an Officer dug a small trench on our right rear, facing South East.

Owing to the mixed nature of the fighting and the number of casualties on the way to the 1st Objective and the fact that the Division on the right did not keep up with our advance, as had been planned, there were insufficient men to go right forward as far as the second Objective without dangerously exposing the whole of the right flank. As it was there was a gap of some 700 yards between the right of the forward part of the East Yorkshire Regiment and the left of the D.L.I., or the Division on the right.

October 4th, about 1 p.m the enemy opened heavy fire on our front and rear lines and appeared to be going to counter attack. Whether he actually started to do so or not is uncertain. The S.O.S. barrage was called for and stopped further trouble for the time being.

At 2.15 p.m. the 1st really serious counter attack began to develop. Heavy barrage fire was opened on our lines and the enemy could be seen forming up in large number in the e vicinity of BECELAERE. The lowest estimate of the number to be seen forming up was 500, and it may have been double that number. This attack was apparently directed against POLDERHOUK CHATEAU and the left of the 5th Divisional frontage. As there was at this time a gap of some 600 yards on the right of the troops which were South East of REUTEL the attack looked somewhat dangerous. However, the S.O.S. barrage was again called for and at the same time long range (over 1,000 yards) machine gun and rifle fire was brought to bear on the enemy. The enemy could not only be seen forming up but was also seen to move off in small 'snake' formation, similar to our own. He must have suffered tremendous casualties from our S.O.S. barrage and from our rifle and machine gun fire, but he commenced to advance. How far he got it was impossible for anyone to see except for those who were actually in front of him. The situation became quiet again about 4.30 p.m. and remained so until 7 p.m. when the S.O.S. Signal was again sent up by the troops on our right. At 8.30 p.m. the situation once more became quiet. The S.O.S. was signalled twice during the night, at about 11 p.m. and at 2.30 a.m. but on neither occasion did any Infantry Action develop on the Battalion Frontage.

During the whole of the 4th October the enemy kept up a heavy fire round Battalion Headquarters at I.15.b.3.8. and BLACKWATCH CORNER and also right back to CLAPHAM JUNCTIO

During the night of the 4/5th a patrol of one Officer and four O.R. were sent into REUTEL and brought back the information that were no troops further forward in REUTEL than the line previously reported and that no enemy troops had been encountered in REUTEL. The enemy were, however, seen in REUTEL on the afternoon of the 5th and it seems probably that he had a certain number who were holding out in REUTEL on the night of the 4/5th and who were reinforced early on the morning of the 5th.

The day of the 5th was quiet on the whole but there was intermittent shelling on the front line and Battalion Headquarters throughout the day.

Communication with the front line was established by means of a lamp and Battn. Headquarters back to Brigade also by lamp.

No counter attack developed during the day of the 5th and on the night of the 5/6th it was found possible to relieve some Officers of the 9th and 10th Bns. by other Officers in the 10th Battalions who had been kept back at Battalion Headquarters. These Officers had already been found very useful in going up to reconnoitre the line and had brought back much valuable information.

Owing to the Commanding Officer of the 9th Bn. K.O.Y.L.I being killed the 9th and 10th Bns. were amalgamated under the command of the Officer Commanding 10th K.O.Y.L.I.

At about 6.30 p.m. on the 5th enemy Infantry were seen advancing on the extreme right of our Brigade Frontage, and the S.O.S. signal was sent up. It was also signalled at the same time by the troops on the left of the Brigade. The Infantry attack never materialised but was completely quelled by our Artillery. By 7 p.m. the front line signalled that all was well.

During the night of the 5/6th there was heavy shelling of the front line but no Infantry Actions took place. During this night strong points had been established by 1st East Yorkshire Regiment round our right flank and connection with the troops on our right had been secured.

The day of the 6th passed quietly and was again spent in reorganising and consolidating the ground already captured.

The Battalion was relieved in the line on the night of the 6/7th and moved to the Railway Embankment at ZILLEBEEKE without casualties. The line was taken over by the 7th Battn. Leicester Regiment.

Lt. Col.
Cmdg. 10th (S) Bn. K. O. Yorkshire L. I.

Army Form C. 2118.

B.W. 27.11
3 sheet

6/51 10th ROYAL
Vol 27

WAR DIARY
or
INTELLIGENCE SUMMARY.
(Erase heading not required.)

Instructions regarding War Diaries and Intelligence
Summaries are contained in F. S. Regs., Part II.
and the Staff Manual respectively. Title pages
will be prepared in manuscript.

Place	Date	Hour	Summary of Events and Information	Remarks and references to Appendices
BREWERY CAMP.	Nov 1st 1917		The Battalion (less H & C Coys) paraded at 2 p.m. and proceeded to RAILWAY EMBANKMENT, ZILLEBEKE where they occupied dug-outs, taking over from the 12/13th N.Fs. as Brigade Reserve. H & C Coys in Reserve as above.	Offrs. Ks. W. 2 (900)
			2nd/Lieut. WILLIAMS ("C" Coy) wounded	O.Rs. 1 19(90)
ZILLEBEKE	2nd "	3.30	Battalion (less H & C Coys) left RAILWAY EMBANKMENT at 3.15 p.m. and proceeded to relieve the 9th R.W.Kent in the front line from JOINER'S REST'n to JUDGE CROSS ROADS. Approximately Battalion Headquarters were at the BUTTE	1
	" "	4 "	DE POLYGONE.	
		5th	Holding the Line. Nothing of great importance took place. The	3
		6th	shelled the front line spasmodically but two	K.4
		7th	2nd/Lt GROVER, killed. Infantry was not active. Our patrols went out every night	W.2 8
		8th	Battalion (less D Coy) when Capt W.R.H.Y, relieved by 6th LEICESTER REG'T and	1 died of wounds
			proceeded to RAILWAY EMBANKMENT, ZILLEBEKE, D Coy remaining at the BUTTE	
			OF POLYGONE.	
ZILLEBEKE	9th		Battalion (less D Coy) proceeded to BREWERY CAMP and "D" Coy to ZILLEBEKE	
BREWERY CAMP	10th		The day was spent in cleaning up and looking Inspection &c.	
	11th		Church Parade was held in the morning and the rest of the day to	
			themselves.	
	12th		Battalion paraded at 9.30 a.m. and proceeded to OTTAWA CAMP, OUDERDOM AREA. Instructions were received that route marches were to take place daily in view of the Division being transferred to the 1st Army by hard route.	
OTTAWA CAMP.	13th		Road March and training	

Army Form C. 2118.

WAR DIARY
or
INTELLIGENCE SUMMARY.
(Erase heading not required.)

Instructions regarding War Diaries and Intelligence Summaries are contained in F.S. Regs., Part. II. and the Staff Manual respectively. Title pages will be prepared in manuscript.

Place	Date	Hour	Summary of Events and Information	Remarks and references to Appendices
OTTAWA CAMP	1/4		Route March and Training	
	2/4			
	3/4			
	9/4		21st Division transferred from 2nd to 1st Army by march route. Battalion paraded at 10.50 am and proceeded to the BERGUIN AREA billeting at NOOTE BOOM. The weather was very fine during the march.	
	1st		Battalion paraded at 10.15 am and continued the march to CAURESQURE occupying civic billets.	
	10th		Battalion paraded at 9 am and continued the march to GONNEHEM where the Battalion paraded at 1 pm. The Divisional Commander Major General Willis inspected the Battalion on the line of march and congratulated the Commanding Officer on the smartness and general appearance of the Company.	
	20th		Battalion paraded at 9 am and continued the march to COURIERE where they occupied huts. Number of other ranks to the camp.	
	21st		Battalion paraded at 10am and continued the march to ECOIVRES (village bath) at 10.15 and Ablution huts.	

A6945 Wt. W11422/M1160 350,000 12/16 D. D. & L. Forms/C./2118/14.

Army Form C. 2118.

WAR DIARY
or
INTELLIGENCE SUMMARY.
(Erase heading not required.)

Instructions regarding War Diaries and Intelligence Summaries are contained in F. S. Regs., Part II. and the Staff Manual respectively. Title pages will be prepared in manuscript.

Place	Date	Hour	Summary of Events and Information	Remarks and references to Appendices
ECOIVRES	22nd		During the whole 5 days marching there was not a single case of a man falling out, and all ranks were in excellent health and spirits. Captains at disposal of Company Commanders for fitting, re-equipping and cleaning up etc.	
	23rd		Musical Inspection of the Battalion and Coys at disposal of Coy Commanders.	
	24th		Rooking for the Battalion and Coys as "the disposal of Coy Commanders"	
	25th		Band parade.	
	26th		Training carried out in accordance with instructions received from Divisional and Brigade	
	27th		Training continued.	
	28th		Training continued. Reinforcement of 100 men arrived, though young, this draft when a comfort one - being well up in drill. (Tuesday) Lewis Gun and Bombing. The physique of the men good as the whole.	
	29th		Training continued.	
	30th		Received warning order for transport to be ready to move at 6 pm and Batln to be called at 4.45am at 7pm a further warning to move at 9am and rendered to Huxleny warning at	

E.G. Parker ℓt. for
Capt & Adjt
ℓt (s) Bn K.O.Y.L.I.

WAR DIARY
INTELLIGENCE SUMMARY

Army Form C. 2118.

10th KOYLI Vol 25
Dec 1917

Place	Date	Hour	Summary of Events and Information	Remarks and references to Appendices
	DECEMBER 1917			
	1st		The Battalion entrained at 2 a.m at SAVY (near AUBIGNY) and detrained at TINCOURT at 1 p.m. Billets were found for the men when orders were received for the Battalion to parade at 3 p.m. in readiness to proceed to the line. Iron rations were issued and then commenced a very tiring march, the roads being congested causing frequent stoppages. Half way through the march a halt was called and tea issued. The Battalion arrived Railway Dugouts (W.23.b.50.05.) at 12 midnight and relieved the 19th Bn. Middlesex Regt.	
	2nd		Remained in Reserve. Very quiet.	
	3rd		Very severe frost set in.	
	4th		Battalion moved off at 11 a.m. to relieve a composite Battalion in the Front Line. Relief was carried out without incident apart from intermittent shelling. The day passed very quietly. During the night a working party was found for the artillery and four 6" Howitzers were successfully moved.	

Army Form C. 2118.

WAR DIARY
or
INTELLIGENCE SUMMARY.
(Erase heading not required.)

Place	Date	Hour	Summary of Events and Information	Remarks and references to Appendices
	DECEMBER 1917			Officers / Other Ranks — K W M / K W M
	5th	about 6 p.m.	about 6 p.m. the Battalion received the 2nd Cavalry Dismounted Battalion which manned the left occupying Railway Embankment from X.13.a.25.40 to X.7.c.1.4. Enemy shelled the entrainment very vigorously in the evening. During the night posts were established in front. A covering party was again provided for the artillery who added two 60 pdrs from gun pits near X.7a.70.90	K / 1 W / 2
	6th		Major R.H.M. SETTLE 9th Hussars joined as second-in-command. Day very quiet. At night work was continued on advanced posts	
	7th		Battalion relieved about 6 p.m. by 15th Bn. D.L.I. and returned to RAILWAY DUGOUTS N.23.T.50.05. Captain WRAY'S company remaining in support in the BROWN LINE	W / 4
	8th		In Reserve	
	9th		Battalion relieved by 12/13th Northumberland Fusiliers went in Divisional Reserve at LONGAVESNES. Accommodation in tents	K / 2
LONGAVESNES	10th		Day occupied in cleaning up and inspections. Lewis party rejoined from HAMEL	

WAR DIARY or INTELLIGENCE SUMMARY

Army Form C. 2118.

Instructions regarding War Diaries and Intelligence Summaries are contained in F.S. Regs., Part II. and the Staff Manual respectively. Title pages will be prepared in manuscript.

(Erase heading not required.)

Place	Date	Hour	Summary of Events and Information	Remarks and references to Appendices
LONGUESNES	11th		Cleaning up continued and running a working party of 2 Officers & 100 other Ranks detailed for work on Bath Line.	Officers K.W.M. R.W.M. Other Ranks
"	12th		Camp moved to a better site. Otherwise the tents have been standing in a sea of mud. Working Party of 2 Officers & 100 O. ranks again detailed.	2
"	13th		Companies at disposal of Company Commanders for training.	
"	14th		Training continued. Recreation for Officers and all O.Rks arrived with Reinforcements.	
"	15th		Batt. Paraded for Physical Training under Bomb Instructor. G.O.C. 64th Bde inspected transport at 10.30 a.m. at 2.15 p.m. G.O.C. presented medal ribbons to C.S.M. STEELE and Pte. SHELDON and CREASER.	
"	16th		Divine Service held in R.F.C. Hangar near camp. Remainder of day – resting. 2/Lieuts. J.W. HERITAGE and G.J. BOWKER joined the Bn. moved off from LONGUESNES at 3 p.m. to relieve 10th YORKSHIRE Regt. in the Front Line. Enemy shelled heavily but no casualties.	

Army Form C. 2118.

WAR DIARY
or
INTELLIGENCE SUMMARY.
(Erase heading not required.)

Instructions regarding War Diaries and Intelligence Summaries are contained in F. S. Regs., Part II. and the Staff Manual respectively. Title pages will be prepared in manuscript.

Place	Date	Hour	Summary of Events and Information	Remarks and references to Appendices
	DEC. 1917			
	17th		were sustained. The guns were shelled intermittently throughout the night. 'B' and 'D' Companies in the front line – VAUCELETTE FARM sector and 'A' and 'C' Coys in support. Thick layer of snow. One shell wounded 6 men.	
	18th		Day was very quiet and Coys were chiefly engaged in improving the trenches and dug-outs. Bn. Hqrs. still shelled at intervals.	2
	19th		Weather very foggy & one small venture 300–400 yards out into "No man's land" without danger. Covering patrols were out all day.	
	20th		Weather still thick and very cold. Very little shelling. The East Yorks extended its line up to BIRCH TREE COPSE and took over part of the line held by the 1st Bn. East Yorks. Regt.	9
	21st		Day very quiet. Battalion relieved by 7th K.O.Y.L.I. and went back to Brigade Reserve at RAILWAY EMBANKMENT W.23.b.50.05 leaving 'A' Coy in the CAVALRY LINE, and 'C' Coy in the BROWN LINE in support.	
	22nd		Remained in Brigade Reserve.	1

WAR DIARY
or
INTELLIGENCE SUMMARY.
(Erase heading not required.)

Army Form C. 2118.

Place	Date	Hour	Summary of Events and Information	Remarks and references to Appendices
	DEC. 1917		Remained in Reserve.	
	23rd		" " "	
	24th		" " " Major R.H.N. SETTLE rejoined from leave.	
	25th		" " "	
	26th		Battalion relieved by 1st. LINCOLN Regt. about 3pm and went into Divl. Reserve at RAILWAY CAMP, HEUDECOURT.	
HEUDECOURT	27th		Day occupied in cleaning up and inspections.	
	28th		Companies at disposal of Coy Commanders for training. all the men were bathed under Battalion arrangements. Sergeants mess held Xmas celebrations.	
"	29th		Training continued. A working party of 4 officers & 100 men was detailed for the defence of HEUDECOURT.	
	30th		Battalion "stood to" at 7.a.m. owing to heavy enemy barrage fire just N. of HEUDECOURT. Xmas dinners at 2pm followed by football match and concert at 6p.m. by Divisional Party.	
	31st		The Battalion moved from RAILWAY CAMP, HEUDECOURT to new camp at SAULCOURT. First anniversary of the Battalion Century	

Army Form C. 2118.

WAR DIARY
or
INTELLIGENCE SUMMARY.
(Erase heading not required.)

Instructions regarding War Diaries and Intelligence Summaries are contained in F. S. Regs., Part II. and the Staff Manual respectively. Title pages will be prepared in manuscript.

Place	Date	Hour	Summary of Events and Information	Remarks and references to Appendices
SAULCOURT	DEC. 1917			Officers O.Ranks
	31		During the year 180,000 francs had been taken and about 10000 francs profit made of which about 9000 francs had been spent on free teas, xmas dinners, games etc.	K W K W M

E.T. Parks, Lieut.
Adjutant
for O.C. 10th (S) Bn. K.O. Yorks. L.I.

Army Form C. 2118.

10th Bn
KOYLI
Vol 29

29.11
6 sheets

WAR DIARY or INTELLIGENCE SUMMARY.
(Erase heading not required.)

Instructions regarding War Diaries and Intelligence Summaries are contained in F. S. Regs., Part II. and the Staff Manual respectively. Title pages will be prepared in manuscript. January 1916

Place	Date	Hour	Summary of Events and Information	Remarks and references to Appendices
SAULCOURT	JANUARY 1916 1st		Battalion in Divisional Reserve. Companies at disposal of Company Commanders. Engaged in improving new camp etc.	
"	2nd		Remained in Reserve.	
"	3rd		" — " — "	
"	4th		Battalion left camp at SAULCOURT at 3pm and relieved 9th Bn. LEICESTER Regt. in night out posts without incident. Companies in position as follows:— 'C' Coy Front Line (2/Lieut DORÉ J.W.) — 'B' Coy Right Support (Captain P.D. ROOKE) — 'D' Coy Left Support (2/Lieut H HUTSON) — 'A' Coy Reserve (2/Lt R.K. JAMES). Captain NAVY had the misfortune to fall and break his wrist and afterwards went to hospital. Very severe frost still continued.	
"	5th		Work was now chiefly clearing trenches of refuse, and general improvement of where they were in very bad need. Protective patrols were out all night about 300 yards in front of our wire.	
"	6th		Work proceeded. Small parties of the enemy observed and fired on by our snipers. Reconnoitring patrol under 2/Lt R.B. BARTER left our line to locate enemy posts. Protective patrols again active.	

Army Form C. 2118.

WAR DIARY
or
INTELLIGENCE SUMMARY.
(Erase heading not required.)

Instructions regarding War Diaries and Intelligence Summaries are contained in F.S. Regs., Part II. and the Staff Manual respectively. Title pages will be prepared in manuscript.

Place	Date	Hour	Summary of Events and Information	Remarks and references to Appendices
	JANUARY 1916			
	7th		Deepening and widening of trenches under supervision of R.E.s. Hostile Artillery very active against EPEHY. 2 Reconnoitring Patrols in charge of N.C.Os., Sgt NINFIELD 'C' Co. complimented by the Brigadier on his report. Thaw and rain made the ground very bad. 2/Lieut DORE admitted to hospital (sickness)	
	8th		Snow very hard in the early morning making the ground very treacherous. Heavy snow towards mid-day in the nature of a blizzard, during which patrols were sent out. Battalion was relieved about 5-30 p.m. by 1st Bn. East Yorks Regt. and went into support in EPEHY — Two Coys ('A' and 'C') in cellars in the village and 'B' and 'D' in dugouts in the RAILWAY EMBANKMENT.	
	9th		Remained in Support. 'B' Coy furnished Working Party on O.T. from Support Line.	
	10th		'B' Coy engaged on Working Party on the O.T. in Left Sub-Sector. 'D' Coy engaged on Working Party on the O.T. in Left out-sector. Weather both — thaw and rain making ground very heavy.	
	11th		Still — support. Capt Neill rejoined the Bn. from sick leave. Battalion	

A6945 Wt. W14422/M1160 350,000 12/16 D. D. & L. Forms/C./2118/14.

Army Form C. 2118.

WAR DIARY
or
INTELLIGENCE SUMMARY.
(Erase heading not required.)

Instructions regarding War Diaries and Intelligence Summaries are contained in F. S. Regs., Part II. and the Staff Manual respectively. Title pages will be prepared in manuscript.

Place	Date	Hour	Summary of Events and Information	Remarks and references to Appendices
EPEHY	JANUARY 1918			
	11th		Headquarters heavily shelled in EPEHY.	
	12th		Battalion relieved the 1st Bn E Yorks Regt in the RIGHT Sub-sector taking over and occupied Keep in the following positions - 'D' Coy Support –	
			Line (Capt NEIN) - 'B' Coy Right Support (Capt ROOTE) - 'D' Coy Left Support –	
			(2/Lt JAMES) - 'C' Coy in Reserve - (2/Lt GREENSHIELDS)	
	13th		Trenches were in a very bad state, owing to rains and men worked trying	
			to clear them. 2/Lt. PRING took out a reconnoitring patrol	
	14th		Working Parties in trenches. 2/Lt PRING went out with 12 OR to obtain	
			in re-wiring the front. 2/Lt PRING went out with 12 OR to obtain	
			identification, but met with no success. 'A' and 'O' Coys changed over	
	15th		Trenches were more than knee deep in mud. Work went on trying	
			to clear them. 2/Lt PRING again went out but met with no better	
			success. Have heavy rains.	
	16th		Owing to the previous bad weather the trenches were now practically	
			untenable, especially the front line, most of the fire steps and shelters	
			having collapsed and men were almost waist deep in mud.	

WAR DIARY or INTELLIGENCE SUMMARY

Army Form C. 2118.

Place	Date	Hour	Summary of Events and Information	Remarks and references to Appendices
	January 1916			
	16th		Battalion relieved by the 1st Bn East Yorks Regt about 6pm and marched back to SAULCOURT	
SAULCOURT	17th		Battalion in Brigade Reserve, cleaning up. 'C' Coy. provided a working party from 6pm to 10pm on C.T. in 1st Sub-Sect.	
"	18th		In Reserve. Engaged in digging trenches round huts and laying paths through the camp. 'B' Coy provided working party on C.T. new bathhouse	
"	19th		In reserve. 'B' Coy working party. Lecture by Capt. FISH R.F.C. on their work.	
"	20th		Relieved by 8th Bn. LEICESTER Regt about 4pm and moved into rest camp in SAULCOURT. Bn now part of Brigade in Reserve.	
"	21st		Companies at disposal of Company Commanders. Three working parties of 50 each working under R.E. tunnellings in 8 hour shifts.	
"	22nd		9 Lewis Gun teams manning anti-aircraft posts. Working parties and Lewis Gun teams were again provided. Remainder of Coys at Coy Commanders disposal. Lecture by the Commanding

Army Form C. 2118.

WAR DIARY
or
INTELLIGENCE SUMMARY.
(Erase heading not required.)

Place	Date	Hour	Summary of Events and Information	Remarks and references to Appendices
	JANUARY 1918			
SAULCOURT	22nd		Officers to Officers on "Treatment of the Men"	
	23rd		The usual anti aircraft L.G. Posts found, and working parties	
			found for R.E. Tunnelling in and around EPEHY	
	24th		Reorganisation of Companies. All Coys to have four Platoons with	
			one Lewis Gun Section in each Platoon. Usual working parties	
			found as for 23rd.	
	25th		Commanding Officer and Coy Cmdrs reconnoitre the BROWN LINE in	
			accordance with Defence Scheme. Working Parties as for	
			24th inst. Capt. E.S.PARTE proceeded to England on special leave	
			for 1 month. Lieut H.C.WALBY returned from leave and took	
			over Adjutancy.	
	26th		Usual Working Parties found as for 25th. Lecture by C.O. to all	
			Officers on "Training of Platoons for Offensive action".	
	27th		Church Parade for C. of E. at 10 a.m. Working Parties as for 26th	
	28th		Usual Working Parties as for previous days.	
	29th		About 7.45 A.M. Rumbles of Guns were heard from the direction of	

Army Form C. 2118.

WAR DIARY
or
INTELLIGENCE SUMMARY.
(Erase heading not required.)

Instructions regarding War Diaries and Intelligence Summaries are contained in F.S. Regs., Part II. and the Staff Manual respectively. Title pages will be prepared in manuscript.

Place	Date	Hour	Summary of Events and Information	Remarks and references to Appendices
SAULCOURT	JANUARY 1918			
	29th		The line and all ranks were on the alert with Box Respirators in alert position to fix gas and alarm extends	
			Working parties as for 29th	
	30th		Tactical schemes for N.C.O. and men in accordance with programme of training and working parties as for previous day	
	31st		as for 30th inst.	

J K Watty
Lieutenant
a/Adjutant
for O.C. 10th Bn. K.O.Y.L.I.

www.ingramcontent.com/pod-product-compliance
Lightning Source LLC
Chambersburg PA
CBHW081536160426

43191CB00011B/1776